*From Notebooks
and Personal Papers*

Rainer Maria Rilke

From Notebooks and Personal Papers

translated from German
by David Need

Shearsman Books

First published in the United Kingdom in 2018 by
Shearsman Books
50 Westons Hill Drive
Emersons Green
BRISTOL
BS16 7DF

Shearsman Books Ltd Registered Office
30–31 St. James Place, Mangotsfield, Bristol BS16 9JB
(this address not for correspondence)

www.shearsman.com

ISBN 978-1-84861-602-8

Contents

Appendices

Introduction

Rainer Maria Rilke (1875–1926) is recognized as one of the great poets of 20th century European modernism. He is best known for a range of works including *Letters to a Young Poet*, *The Book of Hours*, *New Poems* (Rilke's response to early Modernist plastic and visual arts), and the two collections that are considered his masterworks, *The Duino Elegies* and *Sonnets to Orpheus*, completed toward the end of his life, in 1922.

From 1921–1926, Rilke lived in southern Switzerland, in a region called the Valais that constitutes the upper Rhone Valley and its surroundings. Following the completion of the *Elegies* and *Sonnets*, Rilke began to work in both French and German. A collection of French poems addressed to the landscape of Valais, *Quatrains Valaisans*, was published in 1926. In May of that same year, Rilke sent his publishers an arrangement of German-language poems as a possible manuscript; the bulk of these date to 1924, but the collection included both material culled from a recently recovered 1906 daybook and a final set of poems written over the last two years of his life. Rilke sent the last of these in August 1926; he would die of complications from leukemia just four months later.

This volume is the first English translation of these poems in the arrangement Rilke had set down in 1926. A number of the poems have been included in various volumes of selected late poems and all were translated by Leishman (1957) in his running translation of uncollected poems and fragments according to the sequence of these in Insel's 1955 *Complete Works*. The arrangement translated here has only appeared in German as *Aus Taschen-Büchern und Merk-Blättern*, (Insel-Verlag, 1950).[1]

In many ways, this arrangement reflects Rilke's awareness of his illness and likely death. The bulk of the poems come from 1924 following the first onset (in the winter of 1923-4) of what would later be diagnosed as leukemia, and the last ten poems from 1922, 1925 and 1914-5 function as a final coda. The sense of the occasional about the collection as a whole and the at-times stark difficulty of the poetry thus stages an attitude Rilke wished to convey—about his work (and about what work can do), and about our place in death and life.

---

[1] That edition is subtitled "in chance order," but this is to some extent a conceit. The arrangement reflects the order of poems as set down in a notebooks sent to Rilke's publishers, and the inclusion of the material from the 1906 Capri journal and the last poems sent to the Kippenburgs in August 1926 follows the instructions given by Rilke in his letters from that time.

§

This volume presents Rilke's last suite of poems in a bilingual edition. The translation is followed by three appendices designed to give readers background and guide to reading the work. These include an essay that details connections between this collection and Rilke's earlier work, a set of notes on the poems that identifies key motifs and offers translations of earlier settings of these motifs, and an essay on non-dual language and the translator's decision to render *Raum* variously according to context as "space," "room," and "affordance.

From Notebooks and Personal Papers

Herbst

Oh hoher Baum des Schauns, der sich entlaubt:
nun heißts gewachsen sein dem Übermaße
von Himmel, das durch seine Äste bricht.
Erfüllt vom Sommer, schien er tief und dicht,
uns beinah denkend, ein vertrautes Haupt.
Nun wird sein ganzes Innere zur Straße
des Himmels. Und der Himmel kennt uns nicht.

Ein Äußerstes: daß wir wie Vogelflug
uns werfen durch das neue Aufgetane,
das uns verleugnet mit dem Recht des Raums,
der nur mit Welten umgeht. Unsres Saums
Wellen-Gefühle suchen nach Bezug
und trösten sich im Offenen als Fahne—
....
Aber ein Heimweh meint das Haupt des Baums.

(Herbst 1924)

Autumn

Oh loftier tree in our gaze, that scatters its leaves:
now you'd say it had reached the boundlessness
of the sky that breaks through its branches.
Full of summer, it shone, deep and thick,
as if thinking about us—a friendly head.
Now all the inwardness along the streets will be
the sky's. And the sky doesn't know us.

An outermost limit: so that we, like a bird in flight,
throw ourselves through the newly opened-out,
which repudiates us according to the law of affordance
that now surrounds us with World. The wave-feelings
at our seams look for purchase
and console themselves in the open as color—
. . . .
But the homesick are reminded of the head of the tree.

(Autumn, 1924)

…Wenn aus des Kaufmanns Hand
die Waage übergeht
an jenen Engel, der sie in den Himmeln
stillt und beschwichtigt mit des Raumes Ausgleich…

(Val-Mont, in Herbst 1924)

...As if a scale is passed from
the traders' hands
to that angel, who stops it in the
sky and steadies it with the settling of the affordances...

(Valmont, in Autumn, 1924)

Ach, nicht getrennt sein,
nicht durch so wenig Wandung
ausgeschlossen vom Sternen-Maß.
Innres, was ists?
Wenn nicht gesteigerter Himmel,
durchworfen mit Vögeln und tief
von Winden der Heimkehr.

(Paris 1925)

Ah, not to be separated,
not to be closed out from the scope of the
stars by even the slightest screen.
The inward—what is it?
If not an even higher sky,
tossed through with birds and deep
with the winds of homecoming.

(Paris, 1925)

Unaufhaltsam, ich will die Bahn vollenden
mich schreckt es, wenn mich ein Sterbliches hält.
Einmal hielt mich ein Schoß.
Ihm sich entringen, war tödlich:
ich rang mich ins Leben. Aber sind Arme so tief,
sind sie so fruchtbar, um ihnen
durch die beginnliche Not
neuer Geburt zu entgehn?

(Paris 1925)

Ceaselessly, I want to finish this path,
it frightens me when someone mortal stops me.
A mother's lap once held me.
Escaping it was like death:
I wrung myself into life. But are her arms too long,
are they too fruitful, to slip past them
into the beginning-like want
of a new birth?

(Paris, 1925)

Jetzt wär es Zeit, daß Götter träten aus
bewohnten *Dingen*...
Und daß sie jede Wand in meinem Haus
umschlügen. Neue Seite. Nur der Wind,
den solches Blatt im Wenden würfe, reichte hin,
die Luft, wie eine Scholle, umzuschaufeln:
ein neues Atemfeld. Oh Götter, Götter!
Ihr Oftgekommnen, Schläfer in den Dingen,
die heiter aufstehn, die sich an den Brunnen,
die wir vermuten, Hals und Antlitz waschen
und die ihr Ausgeruhtsein leicht hinzutun
zu dem, was voll scheint, unserm vollen Leben.
Noch einmal sei es euer Morgen, Götter.
Wir wiederholen. Ihr allein seid Ursprung.
Die Welt steht auf mit euch, und Anfang glänzt
an allen Bruchstelln unseres Mißlingens....

(Fragmentarisch, Muzot, Herbst 1925)

Now is the time that the gods would step out
of the *things* they had inhabited…
when they would crash off every wall in my
house. A new page. Just the wind,
in which each leaf, tossed in its turning, reaches out,
and fills the air like an ice floe:
a new atmosphere. O gods, gods!
You who had come so often, asleep in *things*,
who arise cheerfully, whom we assume are
there in the fountain, when we wash our neck and face,
and who carelessly add your being-rested
to that which seemed full, our already full lives.
May it once again be as it was in your morning, gods.
We repeat. You are the source of all.
The world arises with you, and origin sparkles
in all the cracks of our mistakes…

(Fragmentary, Muzot, Autumn 1925)

O Lacrimosa

(Trilogie zu einer künftigen Musik von Ernst Krenek)

I

Oh Tränenvolle, die, verhaltner Himmel,
über der Landschaft ihres Schmerzes schwer wird.
Und wenn sie weint, so weht ein weicher Schauer
schräglichen Regens an das Herzens Sandschicht.

Oh Tränenschwere. Waage aller Tränen!
Die sich nicht Himmel fühlte, da sie klar war,
und Himmel sein muß um der Wolken willen.

Wie wird es deutlich und wie nah, dein Schmerzland,
unter der strengen Himmels Einheit. Wie ein
in seinem Liegen langsam waches Antlitz,
das waagrecht denkt, Welttiefe gegenüber.

II

Nichts als ein Atemzug ist das Leere, und jenes
grüne Gefülltsein der schönen
Bäume: ein Atemzug!
Wir, die Angeatmeten noch,
heute noch Angeatmeten, zählen
diese, der Erde, langsame Atmung,
deren Eile wir sind.

O Lacrimosa

(A Trilogy on a Future Piece of Music by Ernst Krenek)

I

Oh, that tearful one, who grows heavy,
a more subdued sky over the landscape of her pain.
And if she cries out, so a shower of slanting rain would
gust across the shifting sands of her heart.

Oh, she who is heavy with tears. The Balanced Scale of all tears!
Who did not feel she was sky, since she was transparent,
and the sky is there for the sake of clouds.

How your pain-land comes into focus and how near,
under the censure of the strict skies. Slowly, like a
watchful face in a bed, that is imagined
to be a balance against the world's depths.

II

Emptiness is nothing but a breath, and that
green fullness of the beautiful
trees: a breath!
We, who still take breath
who still take breath today, reckon
by this slow breathing the earth
through which we hurry.

III

Aber die Winter! Oh diese heimliche
Einkehr der Erde. Da um die Toten
in dem reinen Rückfall der Säfte
Kühnheit sich sammelt,
künftiger Frühlinge Kühnheit.
Wo das Erdenken geschieht
unter der Starre: wo das von den großen
Sommern abgetragene Grün
wieder zum neuen
Einfall wird und zum Spiegel des Vorgefühls;
wo die Farben der Blumen
jenes Verweilen unserer Augen vergißt.

(Paris, Mai oder Juni? 1925)

III

But Winter! Oh the earth's secret
retreat. Since about the dead,
in the pure relapse of the humors,
a boldness gathers,
the boldness of the coming spring.
Where the designs are laid out
under the stars; where the worn-out green
of the vast summer
is again a new
idea and a mirror of portent;
where the color of the flowers
forgets how our eyes lingered.

(Paris, May or June, 1925)

Im Kirchhof zu Ragaz — Niedergeschriebenes

I

Falter, über die Kirchhof-Mauer
herübergeworfen vom Wind,
trinkend aus den Blumen der Trauer,
die vielleicht unerschöpflicher sind...

Falter, der das geopferte Blühen,
das nachdenklicher geschieht,
in das unbedingte Bemühen
aller Gärten einbezieht.

(Ragaz, Juni 1924)

II

TOTEN-MAHL

Unsere Türen schließen sehr fest;
aber die waagrechte Tür,
selbst aus dichtem Porphyr,
läßt
ganz unmerklich zu uns
jene, die schon des Grunds
starke Verwandlung umfaßte:
schwankend und schweigenden Munds
kommen sie langsam zu Gaste...

Decke, Seele, den Tisch,
den sie, in Heimweh, umkreisen,
reiche ihnen die Speisen,
den verschwiegenen Fisch,
den sie berühren im Stehn...

Nine Poems Written in a Churchyard in Ragaz

I

Butterflies, tossed up over
the churchyard-wall on the wind,
sipping at the flowers of mourning
are perhaps more inexhaustible…

Butterflies, for whom the sacrificial flower,
that more thoughtfully appeared,
factors all gardens
into its unconditional striving.

(Ragaz, June 1924)

II

Meal for the Dead

Our doors close so firmly
but the door that faces us,
made of heavy porphyry,
lets in
all that is imperceptible to us, and
this includes the intense transformations
of what is already in the ground:
swaying and mute-lipped
they slowly come as guests…

Lay the cloth, soul, on the table,
for those who, homesick, circle,
lay out the food for them,
the fish that's been saved
just for those that crowd around…

Nichts wird von ihnen vermindert,
alles bleibt heil, doch das hindert
nicht, daß sie grader entgehn.
Sie sind auf Seiten dessen,
was uns vermehrt, unermessen
brauchen nicht Nahrung und Wein;
doch, daß sie's tastend erkannten,
macht sie uns zu Verwandten,—
und die Speise wird rein
von der nötigen Tötung:
sie verlöschen die Rötung
alles tierischen Bluts.
Schaffen uns Künste der Küche
Lockung und Wohlgerüche,
ihre Reinigung tuts.

(Ragaz, Juni 1924)

III

Kennst du das, daß durch das Laubwerk Scheine
fallen in den Schatten, und es weht...
: wie dann in des fremden Lichtes Reine,
kaum geschaukelt, blau und einzeln, eine
hohe Glockenblume steht:

Also bist du, bei den Toten, immer
in ein ausgespartes Licht gestellt,
langsam schwankend... Andre leiden schlimmer.
Und in deinem unbenutzten Schimmer
spielt der Überfluß der Unterwelt.

(Ragaz, Juni 1924)

It won't be too little for them,
it all remains in one piece, yet that doesn't
stop them, since they just go past.
They belong to those who
do not need the nourishment and wine
that strengthens us immeasurably;
but, since they grope about to find it
it makes them our kin,—
and the spread is purified
by the obligatory kill:
they leave behind the redness
of all the animal blood.
The allure and pleasant aromas
the arts of the kitchen create for us
are purgative for *them*.

(Ragaz, June 1924)

III

Do you know this—that through the foliage, coins of light
fall in the shadows, and drift…
: how, then, in the purity of that strange light,
hardly shaking, blue and solitary, a
tall bellflower stands…

There you are, among the dead, always
placed in a recessed light,
slowly swaying… others suffer worse.
And in your unspent shimmering
the abundance of the underworld plays.

(Ragaz, June 1924)

IV

Wir könnten wissen. Leider, wir vermeidens;
verstießen lange, was uns nun verstößt.
Befangen in den Formen unsres Leidens,
begreifen wir nicht mehr, wenn Leid sich löst

und *draußen* ist: als blasser Tag um Schemen,
die selber nicht mehr leiden, sondern nur,
gleichmütig mit der schöpfenden Figur,
das Maß des herrenlosen Leidens nehmen.

(Ragaz, Juni 1924)

V

Unstete Waage des Lebens
immer schwankend, wie selten
wagt ein geschicktes Gewicht
anzusagen die immerfort andre
Last gegenüber.

Drüben, die ruhige
Waage des Todes.
Raum auf den beiden
verschwisterten Schalen.
Gleichviel Raum. Und daneben,
ungebraucht,
all Gewichte des Gleichmuts,
glänzen, geordnet.

(Ragaz, Juni 1924)

IV

We could know. Sadly, we evade it;
for a long time we denied what denies us now.
Prejudiced by the shapes of our sorrows
we no longer understand when grief breaks off

and is *out there*: like a paler day around a silhouette;
we'd no longer suffer, but just,
calmed by a summoning figure,
take on the dimensions of the abandoned suffering.

(Ragaz, June 1924)

V

Unsteady scales of life,
always swaying, as rarely
a skillful weight dares to
accept the always changing
load that gains against it.

On the other hand, the quiet
scales of death.
Room on both
ensistered pans.
Nevertheless Room. And next to it
unused,
all the weights of serenity
gleam, in ranks.

(Ragaz, June 1924)

VI

So leise wie der Druck von deiner Hand
zuweilen war im freudigsten Begegnen:
so kaum beruhend, ist den sehr Entlegnen
der Druck der Luft und jeder Gegenstand.

Die Leiber, die aus der Entweihung heilen,
sind starkere nicht berührend und berührt;
wie Wasser wird ein fließendes Verweilen
durch ihre Schatten durchgeführt.

(Ragaz, Juni 1924)

VII   *Das (Nicht Vorhandene) Kindergrab mit dem Ball*

1)   Von diesen Kreuzen keins,
     nicht Englein, hölzern und zinnern,
     dürften an dich erinnern
     als kleines Ein-mal-eins

     des Todes, den du selber dir deutest:
     sondern, es liege der Ball,
     den du, zu werfen, dich freutest,
     —einfacher Niederfall—

     in einem goldenen Netz
     über der tieferen Truhe.
     Sein Bogen und, nun, seine Ruhe
     befolgen dasselbe Gesetz.

2)   Du warsts imstand und warfst ihn weit hinein
     in die Natur; sie nahm ihn wie den ihren
     und ließ getrost sein Etwas-wärmer-sein
     in ihren sichern Räumen sich verlieren.

VI

So quiet, like the pressure of your hand
occasionally was in joyful greeting:
so barely established, for those quite remote, is
the pressure of the air and every object met.

The bodies, which are healed of their quarrels,
do not lean heavily against each other and yet touch;
like water, a fluent languor would
run through their shadows.

(Ragaz, June 1924)

VII: *A (Non-Existent) Child's Grave with a Ball*

1)   Nothing beside this cross,
       no little angels, wooden or pewter,
       allow us to remember you—
       other than the ABCs

       of death, by which you indicate yourself:
       but, a ball lies there,
       which you were pleased to throw,
       —a simple falling shot—

       in a golden net
       above the deeper coffin.
       Its arch and, now, its rest
       follow the same rule.

2)   You were in good shape and threw it far off
       into nature: she took it as if it was hers
       and its being a bit warmer gave it the confidence
       to disappear into its own safeguarded affordance.

Dann kam er wieder, himmlisch abgekühlt:
wie hast du, ihm entgegen, froh beklommen,
das Übermaß in seinem Wiederkommen
mit allem Übermaß zugleich gefühlt.

3) Wir warfen dieses Ding, das uns gehört,
    in das Gesetz aus unserm, dichten Leben,
    wo immer wieder Wurf und Sturz sich stört.

    Da schwebt es hin und zieht in reinem Strich
    die Sehnsucht aus, die wir ihm mitgegeben—,
    sieht uns zurückgeblieben, wendet sich
    und meint, im Fall, der zunimmt, uns zu heben.

(Ragaz, Juni 1924)

VIII

Das Spiel, da man sich an die Bäume stellt,
um mit einander rasch den Platz zu tauschen:
wars nicht ein letztes Suchen und Belauschen
der einmal innerlich bewohnten Welt?

Sie sprangen fast wie aus den Bäumen vor:
erregte Mädchen in gekreuzter Helle…
Und wer im Wechseln seinen Platz verlor,
den was der Liebesgott und ohne Stelle.

Die Mitte, die nach allen Seiten schreckt,
die Wahl die zuckt, das Zücken aller Schritte—,
und wie von Göttlicherem angesteckt,
war jede innen beides: Baum und Mitte.

(Ragaz, Juni 1924)

Then it came back, cooled like the sky:
as you, facing it, apprehensively happy,
felt the abundance of its return
in the midst of all abundance.

3)   We threw this *thing*, that belongs to us
     according to the rule of our heavy lives,
     while ever again toss and stumble interfere.

     It sweeps off there and, in a straight line, pulls
     the longing that we sent after it—,
     it sees us stay behind, turns back
     and intends, in falling, as it grows larger, to lift us.

(Ragaz, June 1924)

VIII

The game where one stands among the trees
so as to trade places quickly with each other:
wasn't that the last Hide and Seek
of the first inwardly-lived world?

They almost leapt out, as if from behind the trees:
excited girls, in a cruciform brightness…
And the one who lost his place in the exchange,
was Eros—he had no place to stand.

He was the one in the center, who startles in all directions
who sidles at the choice, the pull of every footstep—,
and, as if infected by what was more godly,
both were affected by the other: Tree and center.

(Ragaz, June 1924)

IX

Sterne, Schläfer und Geister
sind nicht verbunden genug;
nächtlich ordnet der Meister
ihren geplanten Bezug.

Über dem schlafenden Plane
zieht er die Linien aus,
wenn das bei Tage Getane
abstirbt im ängstlichen Haus.

Nur in die Liebenden reichen
seine Zeichen hinein,
weil sie, in Träumen voll Teichen,
Blume spiegeln und Stein.

Während Entwürfe ihm keimen,
wirft er, wie Vogelschwung,
Spiegelbild des Geheimen
durch den Glanz ihrer Spiegelung.

(Muzot, 1924)

IX

Stars, sleepers and spirits
are not sufficiently connected;
each night the master orders
their plotted relations.

He traces the lines
over the slumbering blankets,
when what is done by day
dies in the anxious house.

Only in lovers is his
sign enough,
because they, in dreams full of ponds,
reflect flower and stone.

Even as the designs stir in him
he throws, like a flock a birds,
the mirror of what's hidden
through the glimmer of their reflections.

(Muzot, 1924)

Magie

Aus unbeschreiblicher Verwandlung stammen
solche Gebilde—: Fühl! und glaub!
Wir leidens oft: zu Asche werden Flammen,
doch, in der Kunst: zur Flamme wird der Staub.

Hier ist Magie. In das Bereich des Zaubers
scheint das gemeine Wort hinaufgestuft…
und ist doch wirklich wie der Ruf des Taubers,
der nach der unsichtbaren Taube ruft.

(Muzot, Herbst 1924)

Magic

From an indescribable transformation comes
such a shape.—: Feel it! And believe!
We often suffer: what burns becomes ash,
but in this art: dust becomes flame.

Here is magic. In the spell's sphere
the ordinary word appears layered...
and nevertheless real, like the call of a deaf man
who calls to an invisible deaf woman.

(Muzot, Autumn 1924)

Nachthimmel und Sternenfall

Der Himmel, groß, voll herrlicher Verhaltung,
ein Vorrat Raum, ein Übermaß von Welt.
Und wir, zu ferne für die Angestaltung,
zu nahe für die Abkehr hingestellt.

Da fällt ein Stern! Und unser Wunsch an ihn,
bestürzten Aufblicks, dringend angeschlossen:
Was ist begonnen, und was ist verflossen?
Was ist verschuldet? Und was ist verziehn?

(Muzot, Herbst 1924)

Night Sky and Star-Fall

The sky, so great, full of glorious restraint,
a storeroom, an overflow of world.
And we, too distant for the display, are
too close to turn away.

There, a star falls! And our wish on it,
in an upward gaze of dismay, so urgent for connection:
What has begun, and what is bygone?
Who is in debt? And what has spoiled?

(Muzot, Autumn 1924)

Nicht um-stoßen, was steht!
Aber das Stehende stehender,
aber das Wehende wehender
zuzugeben,—gedreht

zu der Mitte des Schauenden,
der es im Schauen preist,
daß es sich am Vertrauenden
jener Schwere entreißt,

drin die Dinge, verlorener
und gebundener, fliehn—,
bis sie, durch uns, geborener,
sich in die Spannung beziehn.

(Muzot, 1924)

What stands, isn't pushed around!
But to admit the stalwart standing,
but to admit the drifter
drifting—rotates

in the midst of the crowd,
who praise it in their look,
so that it snatches to itself
a trust in each weight,

into which *things*, more lost
and more confined, flee—,
until they, who through us have been more
fully born, relate to each other in the tension.

(Muzot, 1924)

Welt was in dem Antlitz der Geliebten—,
aber plötzlich ist sie ausgegossen:
Welt ist draußen. Welt ist nicht zu fassen.

Warum trank ich nicht, da ich es aufhob,
aus dem vollen, dem geliebten Antlitz
Welt, die nah war, duftend meinem Munde?

Ach, ich trank. Wie trank ich unerschöpflich.
Doch auch ich war angefüllt mit zu viel
Welt, und trinkend ging ich selber über.

(Ragaz, Juni 1924: See-Anlage)

World was in the face of the beloved—,
but all of a sudden it poured out:
world is outside, world cannot be caught.

Why didn't I drink, when I lifted it up
from the fullness, from the beloved face-
world, that was close and fragrant to my mouth?

Oh, I drank. How I drank inexhaustibly.
But I was also filled by too much
world, and, drinking, I overwhelmed myself.

(Ragaz, June 1924—Seaside Park)

Garten-Nacht

Nebelnd schweben durch den Rosenbogen,
den man für die Lebenden gebeugt,
jene, die, nicht völlig überzeugt,
aus dem nahen Tod herüberwogen...

Sie, die, diese Erde tief besitzen,
grüßen ihre Oberfläche kühl,—
hoffen, an dem Dörnicht sich zu ritzen
mit vergessnem Schmerzgefühl.

Eine tastet an dem Rebengange
nach dem überraschten Blatt...
Blatt versagt... nun sucht sie mit der Wange...
Aber Nachtwind will an wangesstatt...

(Muzot, Sommer 1924)

Garden Night

Fog drifts through the rose arch
that someone made for the living,
each of whom, is not completely convinced,
by its approach, that death prevails here.

They, who have taken Earth so deeply,
greet the chill on their face—
hope, to be caught on the thorns
by a forgotten grief.

Each traces along the vine's course
for the unexpected flower...
the flower wilts... now they press it to their cheek...
but instead of a cheek, the night wind wants a...

(Muzot, Summer 1924)

Aus dem Umkreis: Nächte

Gestirne der Nacht, die ich erwachter gewahre,
überspannen sie nur das heutige, meine Gesicht,
oder zugleich das ganze Gesicht meiner Jahre,
diese Brücken, die ruhen auf Pfeilern von Licht?

Wer will dort wandeln? Für wen bin ich Abgrund und Bachbett,
daß er mich so im weitesten Kreis übergeht—,
mich überspringt und mich nimmt wie den Läufer im Schachbrett
und auf seinem Siege besteht?

(Muzot, Sommer-Herbst?—1924)

From the Materials for 'Nights'

Stars of the night, that, waking, I begin to see—
Do they throw this bridge across my face on just this day
or, does it cross all the faces of my year in the same moment,
this bridge, that rests on pillars of light?

Who wants to walk there? For whom am I chasm and stream bed,
so that he would go on past my farthest orbit—,
would jump me and take me like a bishop on a chessboard
and stand forth in his victory?

(Muzot—Summer/Autumn? 1924)

Handinneres

Innres der Hand. Sohle, die nicht mehr geht
als auf Gefühl. Die sich nach oben hält
und im Spiegel
himmlische Straßen empfängt, die selber
wandelnden.
Die gelernt hat, auf Wasser zu gehn,
wenn sie schöpft,
die auf den Brunnen geht,
aller Wege Verwandlerin.
Die auftritt in anderen Händen,
die ihresgleichen
zur Landschaft macht:
wandert und ankommt in ihnen,
sie anfüllt mit Ankunft.

(Muzot, Herbst 1924)

The Palm of the Hand

The palm of the hand. Sole, which goes no further
than what is felt. That stops itself on the surface
and in play
welcomes the sky-like streets one
walks.
That has learned to walk on water
when it scoops
all the ways of transformation
from a well.
That appears in another hand,
making its likeness
into a landscape:
it wanders and reaches those
it fills with arrival.

(Muzot, Autumn 1924)

Aus dem Umkreis: Nächte

Nacht. Oh du in Tiefe gelöstes
Gesicht an meinem Gesicht.
Du, meines staunenden Anschauns größtes
Übergewicht.

Nacht, in meinem Blicke erschauernd,
aber in sich so fest;
unerschöpfliche Schöpfung, dauernd
über dem Erdenrest;

voll von jungen Gestirnen, die Feuer
aus der Flucht ihres Saums
schleudern ins lautlose Abenteuer
des Zwischenraums:

wie, durch dein bloßes Dasein, erschein ich,
Übertrefferin, klein—;
doch, mit der dunkelen Erde einig,
wag ich es, in dir zu sein.

(Muzot, Herbst 1924)

From the Materials for "Nights"

Night. O, you, unfolded in the deep,
face against my face.
You, too-vast preponderance of my astonished
gaze.

Night, trembling in my glance,
but so self-sufficient;
inexhaustible Creation, constant
over the rest of the Earth;

full of young stars, the flames
of the flight of their skirts
are flung out into the silent adventure
of the affordant in-between:

as if, through your mere being, I appear,
Outstripped, small—;
but, at one with the dark earth,
I dare—to be in you.

(Muzot, Autumn 1924)

Schwerkraft

Mitte, wie du aus allen
dich ziehst, auch noch aus Fliegenden dich
wiedergewinnst, Mitte, du Stärkste.

Stehender: wie ein Trank den Durst
durchstürzt ihn die Schwerkraft.

Doch aus dem Schlafenden fällt,
wie aus lagernder Wolke
reichlicher Regen der Schwere.

(Muzot, Herbst 1924)

Gravity

Midst, how you extend from
everything—you even reclaim yourself
from those in flight, Midst, you who are strongest.

Someone stands: gravity plunges through
him like a drink plunges through thirst.

He falls into sleep anyway,
the way severity's more abundant rain
falls from a more stationary cloud.

(Muzot, Autumn 1924)

Aus Einem Alten Taschenbuche (1906)

Improvisationen aus dem capreser Winter

Täglich stehst du mir steil vor dem Herzen,
Gebirge, Gestein,
Wildnis, Un-weg: Gott, in dem ich allein
steige und falle und irre…, täglich in mein
gestern Gegangenes wieder hinein
kreisend.
Weisend greift mich manchmal am Kreuzweg der Wind
wirft mich hin, wo ein Pfad beginnt,
oder es trinkt mich ein Weg im Stillen.
Aber dein unbewältigter Willen
zieht die Pfade zusammn wie Alaun,   ?????
bis sie, als alte haltlose Rillen,
sich verlieren ins Abgrundsgraun…

Laß mich, laß mich, die Augen geschlossen,
wie mit verschluckten Augen, laß
mich, den Rücken an den Kolossen,
warten, an deinem Rande, daß
dieser Schwindel, mit dem ich verrinne
meine hingerissenen Sinne
wieder an ihre Stelle legt.
Regt sich den Alles in mir? Ist kein Festes
das bestünde auf seines Gewichts
Anrecht? Mein Bangestes und mein Bestes…
Und der Wirbel nimmt es wie nichts
mit in die Tiefen…

From an Old Notebook (1906)

Improvisations from a Winter in Capri

Each day, you stand above me, steep before the heart—
mountain, crag,
wilderness, trackless: God for whom I climb
everything and fall and wander off... each day, circling
again through what I did
yesterday.
Sometimes it's that you take me at the crossroads of the wind
and drop me, where a path begins,
or that you drink a path into silence for me.
But your more unmastered will
melds the paths together like alum,
until they, older than the unrestrained rills,
fade away in abyssal grey...

Allow me. Allow me, eyes closed,
as if my eyes had been eaten, Allow
me to cling to the ridge of the
colossus, to your rim, so that
this dizziness, with which I unravel
my enraptured desire,
sets me again against its stars.
What then stirs everything in me? Is there nothing of festival
that exists in the claim of this
heaviness? What most frightens me and what I like best...
And the vortex takes it, as if there were nothing
in the deep...

Gesicht, mein Gesicht:
wessen bist du? für was für Dinge
bist du Gesicht?
Wie kannst du Gesicht "sein" für so ein Innen,
drin sich immerfort das Beginnen
mit dem Zerfließen zu etwas ballt.
Hat der Wald ein Gesicht?
Steht der Berge Basalt
gesichtlos nicht da?
Hebt sich das Meer
nicht ohne Gesicht
aus dem Meergrund her?
Spiegelt sich nicht der Himmel drin,
ohne Stirn, ohne Mund, ohne Kinn?

Kommen einem die Tiere nicht
manchmal, als bäten sie: nimm mein Gesicht?
Ihr Gesicht ist ihnen zu schwer,
und sie halten mit ihm ihr klein-
wenig Seele zu weit hinein
ins Leben. Und wir?
Tiere der Seele, verstört
von allem in uns, noch nicht
fertig zu nichts, wir weidenden
Seelen,
flehen wir zu dem Bescheidenden
nächtens nicht um das Nicht-Gesicht,
das zu unserem Dunkel gehört?

Face, my face:
whose are you? For what kind of *thing*
are you face?
As if you, face, could be for an inwardness
in which beginning is constantly
bound up with going off somewhere else.
Do the woods have a face?
Don't the basalt mountains stand
there faceless?
Doesn't the sea rise up here
from its depth
without a face?
Isn't the sky reflected in it,
without a brow, without a mouth, without a chin?

Don't the animals come to people
sometimes as if to ask: can you use my face?
Their face is too difficult for them,
and, in it, they hold their small,
little souls too-far out
into life. And we?
Animals-with-souls, disturbed
by everything that's in us, having
completed nothing — we whose souls have been
put out to graze,
don't we still ask the comforters,
at night about the not-having-any-face[2]
that belongs to our darkness?

---

[2] See *Beginning of Terror*, pp. 27-30 & Rainer Maria Rilke's *Gedichte an Die Nacht* p. 179.

Mein Dunkel, mein Dunkel, da steh ich mit dir,
und alles geht draußen vorbei:
und ich wollte, mir wüchse, wie einem Tier,
eine Stimme, ein einziger Schrei
für alles—. Denn was soll mir die Zahl
der Worte, die kommen und fliehen,
wenn ein Vogellaut, vieltausendmal,
geschrien und wieder geschrien,
ein winziges Herz so weit macht und eins
mit dem Herzen der Luft, mit dem Herzen des Hains
und so hell und so hörbar für ihn…:
der immer wieder, sooft es tagt,
aufsteigt: steilstes Gestein.
Und türm ich mein Herz auf mein Hirn und mein
Sehnen darauf und mein Einsamsein:
wie bleibt das klein,
weil *Er* es überragt.

(1906)

My darkness, my darkness, I stand here with you.
and everything goes by out there;
and I wanted to lick myself, like an animal
a mute, one who cries alone
about everything—. What then should the count
of words be to me, the going towards and fleeing,
if many thousands of times, a bird's call
screeched and screeched again,
so opened a small heart, the call of one
with the air's heart, with the grove's heart,
and so bright and so audible to Him.... :
who, ever again, whenever it dawns,
rises up: the steepest cliff.
And I pile my heart on my head and my
longing on that and my being alone:
how little of that remains
because *He* overtowers it.

(1906)

Wie wenn ich, unter Hundertem, mein Herz,
das überhäufte, lebend wiederfände,
und wieder nähm ich es in meine Hände,
es findend unter Hundertem, mein Herz:
und hübe es hinaus aus mir, in das,
was draußen ist, in grauen Morgenregen,
dem Tage hin, der sich auf langen Wegen
besinnt und wandelt ohne Unterlaß,
oder an Abenden, der Nacht entgegen
der nahenden, der klaren Karitas...

Und hielte es, soweit ich kann, hinein
in Wind und Stille: wenn ich nicht mehr kann,
nimmst du es dann?
Oh nimm es, pflanz es ein!
Nein, wirf es nur auf Felsen, auf Granit,
wohin es fällt; sobald es dir entfallen,
wird es schon treiben und wird Wurzelkrallen
einschlagen in das härteste von allen
Gebirgen, welches sich dem Jahr entzieht.
Und treibt es nicht, ist es nicht jung genug,
wird es allmählich von dem Höhenzug
die Art und Farbe lernen vom Gestein
und wird daliegen unter seinen Splittern,
mit ihm verwachsen und mit ihm verwittern
und mit ihm stehen in den Sturm hinein.

Und willst du's niederlassen in den Grund
der dumpfen Meere, unter Muschelschalen,
wer weiß, ob nicht aus seinem Röhrenmund
ein Tier sich streckt, das dich mit seinen Strahlen
zu fassen sucht und einzuziehen und
mit dir zu schlafen.

How, if I belabored my heart—worth less
than a dollar—I'd find it was alive again,
and I would take my heart again in my hand,
finding it to be less than a dollar:
and it would rise out of me, into
what is beyond it, into the grey morning rain,
out into the day, would reflect on
long walks and roam without a break,
or, in the evenings, would walk toward the night
that approaches, that clear *caritas*...

And, as long as I could, I would hold it, sheltered
in the wind and stillness; and when I couldn't do that any more,
would you then take it?
Oh, take it, plant it someplace!
No, just throw it on the cliffs, on granite,
where it falls; as soon as you drop it,
it will be so driven and will twist its
clinging roots into the hardest of all
mountains, into which it will withdraw for a year.
And it won't strive to push up, it isn't young enough,
it will gradually learn from the mountain range
the type and color of the rock
and will lie there among its splinters,
to bleach with it and to be weathered with it
and to stand with it in the midst of the storm.

And should you settle down into the bed
of the gloomy sea, under the clam shells,
who knows, whether or not a creature stretches
out its tube-like mouth so as to take hold
of you with its ray-like palps, that tries
to draw these tight so as to sleep with you.

... laß nur irgendwo
es eine Stelle finden und nicht so
in Raume sein, dem deine Sterne kaum
genügen können. Sieh, es fällt im Raum.

Du sollst es ja nicht, wie das Herz von Tieren,
in deiner Hand behalten, Nacht und Tag;
wenn es nur eine Weile drinnen lag!

Du konntest in den dürftigsten Verschlag
die Herzen deiner Heiligen verlieren,
sie blühten drin und brachten dir Ertrag.
....
Du freier, unbegreiflicher Verschwender,
da jagst du, wie im Sprung, an mir vorbei.
Du heller Hirsch! Du alter Hundert-Ender!
Und immer wieder wirfst du ein Geweih
von deinem Haupte ab und flüchtest leichter
durch deine Jäger, (wie dich alles trägt!)
sie aber sehen nur, du Unerreichter,
daß hinter dir die Welt zusammenschlägt.

(1906)

....may it somewhere find
a simple place, and may it not be
in the spaces that your stars
barely fill. See, it falls through space.

You shouldn't hold it night and day
in your hand like an animal's heart;
if it could only lay down inside for just a little while!

You were able to shed the hearts of
your saints in the meanest shack,
they flowered there and brought you a yield.
. . . .
You, freer, incomprehensible spendthrift,
there you run, as if in a bound to surpass me.
You brighter stag! You older hundred-pointed one!
And ever again you grow out a set of antlers
on your head and flee quickly
past your hunters, (as if to pull everything to yourself!)
but all they see, unequalled one,
is the world crashing together there behind you.

(1906)

So viele Dinge liegen aufgerissen
von raschen Händen, die sich auf der Suche
nach dir verspäteten: sie wollten wissen.

Und manchmal ist in einem alten Buche
ein unbegreiflich Dunkles angestrichen.
Da warst du einst. Wo bist du hin entwichen?

Hielt einer dich, so hast du ihn zerbrochen,
sein Herz blieb offen, und du warst nicht drin;
hat je ein Redender zu dir gesprochen,
so war es atemlos: Wo gehst du hin?

Auch mir geschahs. Nur, daß ich dich nicht frage.
Ich diene nur und dränge dich um nichts.
Ich halte, wartend, meines Angesichts
williges Schauen in den Wind der Tage
und klage den Nächten nicht...
                              (da ich sie wissen seh)

(1906)

So many *things* lie torn open
by rash hands, in search of
you, who were delayed: they want to know.

And sometimes in an old book,
an inconceivable darkness was painted.
You were the first one there. Where did you escape to?

Someone held you, so you smashed him,
his heart stayed open, but you weren't inside;
each had an advocate to speak to you,
but he lost his breath: where did you go to?

That's what happened to me as well. Only I did not ask after you like that.
I just tried to be of use and pressed you about nothing.
Waiting, I cast the willing glances
of my search in the winds of the days
and do not cry in the night…
                              (There, I see they know)

(1906)

(Vermutlich: für die junge Gräfin M. zu S.)

Nun schließe deine Augen: daß wir nun
dies alles so verschließen dürfen
in unsrer Dunkelheit, in unserm Ruhn,
(wie einer, dems gehört).
Bei Wünschen, bei Entwürfen,
bei Ungetanem, das wir einmal tun,
da irgendwo in uns, ganz tief
ist nun auch dies; ist wie ein Brief,
den wir verschließen.

Laß die Augen zu. Da ist es nicht,
da ist jetzt nichts, als Nacht;
die Zimmernacht rings um ein kleines Licht,
(du kennst sie gut).
Doch *in* dir ist nun alles dies und wacht —
und trägt dein sanft verschlossenes Gesicht
wie eine Flut...

Und trägt nun dich. Und alles in dir trägt,
und du bist wie ein Rosenblatt gelegt
auf deine Seele, welche steigt.
Warum ist das so viel für uns: *zu sehn*?
Auf einem Felsenrand zu stehn?
Wen meinten wir, indem wir *das* begrüßten
was vor uns dalag?...
                              Ja, was war es denn?
Schließ inniger die Augen und erkenn
es langsam wieder: Meer um Meer,
schwer von sich selbst, blau aus sich her
und leer am Rand, mit einem Grund auf Grün.
(Aus welchem Grün? Es kommt sonst nirgends vor...)
Und plötzlich, atemlos, daraus empor
die Felsen jagend, von so tief, daß sie
im steilen Steigen gar nicht wissen, wie

(Presumably for the Young Countess M. zu S.)

Come, shut your eyes: so that we now
are free to seal everything
in our darkness, in our rest
(we alone, who hear it).
It is through petitions, through plans
through not doing anything, that we do something,
so that somewhere in us, in the utter depths
this now also exists: its like a letter,
that we seal.

Keep your eyes shut. *There* is nothing,
right now there is nothing but night;
the dark in the room surrounds a small light,
(you know it well).
But now all this is *in* you and lies awake—
and takes the weight of your gently closed face
like a tide...

And now bears you up. And all is borne in you,
and you are like a rose petal laid
on your soul, that stirs.
Why is that so important to us: *to see*?
To look out from a cliff's edge?
What did we mean to do, when we welcomed *what*
lies there in front of us?...
                                    Yes, what was it then?
Shut your eyes more tightly and slowly
look at it again: sea surrounding sea,
heavy with itself, blue here
and empty at the horizon, with green in the depths.
(What kind of green? It never occurs anywhere else...)
And suddenly, breathless, cliffs, pushed
upwards, from such depths, whose
steep climbs are inconceivable, as if

ihr Steigen enden soll. Auf einmal bricht
es an den Himmeln ab, dort, wo es dicht
von zuviel Himmel ist. Und drüber, sieh,
ist wieder Himmel, und bis weit hinein
in jenes Übermaß: wo ist er nicht?
Strahlen ihn nicht die beiden Klippen aus?
Malt nicht sein Licht das fernste Weiß, den Schnee,
der sich zu rühren scheint und weit hinaus
die Blicke mitnimmt. Und er hört nicht auf,
Himmel zu sein, eh wir ihn atmen.

Schließ, schließ fest die Augen.
War es dies?
Du weißt es kaum. Du kannst es schon nicht mehr
von deinem Innern trennen.
Himmel im Innern läßt sich schwer
erkennen.
Da geht das Herz und geht und sieht nicht her.

Und doch, du weißt, wir können also so
am Abend zugehn, wie die Anemonen,
Geschehen eines Tages in sich schließend,
und etwas größer morgens wieder aufgehn.
Und so zu tun, ist uns nicht nur erlaubt,
das ist es, was wir sollen: Zugehn lernen
über Unendlichem.

(Sahst du den Hirten heut? Der geht nicht zu.
Wie sollte er's? Dem fließt
der Tag hinein und fließt ihm wieder aus
wie einer Maske, hinter der es Schwarz ist...)

Wir aber dürfen uns verschließen, fest
zuschließen und bei jenen dunkeln Dingen,
die längst schon in uns sind, noch einen Rest
von anderm Unfaßbaren unterbringen
wie einer, dems gehört.

(1906)

they went straight up. All at once
they break off at the sky, there, where they
are denser than the so much vaster sky. And up above, see,
it's the sky again, that widens so far
over these floods: where couldn't it be?
Don't both cliffs drop away from it?
May you paint the light that is not theirs the most intense white, that of snow,
that, stirred from within, shines and takes
our glances out into the vast. And it doesn't cease
being the sky when we breathe it.

Shut your eyes, shut them fast.
What is this you see?
You don't know it at all. You cannot keep it really separate from
your inwardness anymore.
The sky that is allowed in your inwardness is
so difficult to recognize.
So, the heart goes and goes and sees nothing before it.

And yet, you know, we could just
approach that open sky in the evening, like an anemone,
over in one day and sealed in ourselves,
and on some larger morning opened again.
But, to be like that is not ever permitted to us,
so that it is what we should do: to learn approach
in relation to the infinite.

(Did you see the shepherd today? He did not close like that.
How chould he? The day flows
into him and leaks out of him again.
as if he wore a mask, behind which it is black…)

But we must shut ourselves away, securely
locked up and, near those dark *things*,
that for a very long time were in us, someday
be given a rest from other incomprehensible matters,
as if one could, in that way, belong.

(1906)

Die Nacht der Frühlingswende
(Capri, 1906)

Ein Netz von raschen Schattenmaschen schleift
über aus Mond gemachte Gartenwege,
als ob Gefangenes sich drinnen rege,
das ein Entfernter groß zusammengreift.

Gefangner Duft, der widerstrebend bleibt.
Doch plötzlich ists, als risse eine Welle
das Netz entzwei an einer hellen Stelle,
und alles fließt dahin und flieht und treibt…

Noch einmal blättert, den wir lange kannten,
der weite Nachtwind in den harten Bäumen;
doch drüber stehen, stark und diamanten,
in tiefen feierlichen Zwischenräumen,
die großen Sterne einer Frühlingsnacht.

The Night of the Spring Equinox
(Capri 1906)

A net of brisk shadow-stitches trails
from the moon, taking over the garden paths
as if they were prisoners muttering in hushed tones,
a vast net that a Distant One draws together.

Air of captivity, that unwillingly remains.
But suddenly it's as if a wave tore
the net apart at an illuminated place,
and everything flowed out and fled and sprouted…

The night wind, that we've long known,
once again batters at the weathered trees;
yet above, strong and diamond-like,
in the deep, solemn in-between spaces, stand
the great stars in the equinoctial night.

Der Goldschmied

Warte! Langsam! droh ich jedem Ringe
und vertröste jedes Kettenglied:
später, draußen, kommt das, was geschieht.
Dinge, sag ich, Dinge, Dinge, Dinge!
wenn ich schmiede; vor dem Schmied
hat noch keines irgendwas zu sein
oder ein Geschick auf sich zu laden.
Hier sind alle gleich, von Gottes Gnaden:
ich, das Gold, das Feuer und der Stein

Ruhig, ruhig, ruf nicht so, Rubin!
Diese Perle leidet, und es fluten
Wassertiefen im Aquamarin.
Dieser Umgang mit euch Ausgeruhten
ist ein Schrecken: alle wacht ihr auf!
Wollt ihr Bläue blitzen? Wollt ihr bluten?
Ungeheuer funkelt mir der Hauf.

Und das Gold, es scheint mit mir verständigt;
in der Flamme hab ich es gebändigt,
aber reizen muß ichs um den Stein.
Und auf einmal, um den Stein zu fassen,
schlägt das Raubding mit metallnem Hassen
seine Krallen in mich selber ein.

(Paris, 1906)

The Goldsmith

Wait! Slowly now! I crimp each link
and lengthen each chain:
later, over there, will be the result.
Thing, I say, *thing, thing, thing*!
As I forge; in front of the smith
even nothing has to be something
or a destiny has to be laid on it.
Here, everything is equal, by God's mercy:
I, the gold, the fire and the stone.

Quietly, quietly, don't shout so, Ruby.
This pearl is tortured, and the deep waters
in the aquamarine flood it.
This close work with the way each of you are patient
is a terror: everything waits on you!
Will you flash blue? Will you bleed?
The cluster flashes impressively at me.

And the gold, it appears to commune with me;
I have tamed it in the flame,
but I have to urge it around the stone.
And suddenly, when I grip the stone,
the coveted thing, with metallic hatred
strikes its claws into me instead.

(Paris, 1906)

Wie Blicke blendend, wie eine warme Arene,
vom Tage bevölkert, umgab dich das Land;
bis endlich strahlend, als goldene Pallas-Athene
auf dem Vorgebirg der Untergang stand,

verstreut von dem groß ihn vergeudenden Meer.
Da wurde Raum in den langsam sich leerenden Räumen;
über dir, über den Häusern, über den Bäumen,
über den Bergen wurde es leer.

Und dein Leben, von dem man die lichten Gewichte gehoben,
stieg, soweit Raum war, über das Alles nach oben,
füllend die rasch sich verkühlende Leere der Welt.
Bis es, im Steigen, in kaum zu erfühlender Ferne
sanft an die Nacht stieß. Da wurden ihm einige Sterne,
als nächste Wirklichkeit, wehrend entgegengestellt.

(Paris/Capri? 1906/1907?)

Like a bedazzled eye, like a warm areola,
the land, crowded by day, surrounded you;
until, radiant at last, doom stands like
Pallas-Athene on the foothills,

scattered widely by the great squandering sea.
Space appeared there in the slowly emptying spaces;
above you, above the houses, above the trees,
above the hills, it became empty.

And your life, its light weight lifted by someone,
rose—so vast was the space—over everything up above,
filling the rapidly cooling emptiness of the world.
Until, in its rise, towards the distance which could barely be felt,
it pushed up gently against the night. Several stars were counter-posed
against it, as the nearest real things.

(Paris/Capri 1906/1907?)

Die Auslage des Fischhändlers

Auf leicht geneigter Marmorplatte liegen sie in Gruppen, manche auf dem feuchten Stein, mit ein wenig schwärzlichem Moos unterlegt, andre in von Nässe dunkelgewordenen flachen Spankörben. Silbern beschuppte, darunter einer, rund nach oben gebogen, wie ein Schwertarm in einem Wappen, so daß das Silber an ihm sich spannt und schimmert. Silbern beschuppte, die quer-über liegen, wie aus altem Silber, schwärzlich beschlagen und drüber einer, der das Maul voran, zurückzukommen scheint, entsetzt, aus dem Haufen hinter ihm. Hat man erst einmal sein Maul gemerkt, so sieht man, da und da, noch eines, ein anderes, rasch hergewendet, klagend. (Was man »klagend« nennen möchte, entsteht wohl, weil hier die Stelle, von der Stimme ausgeht, sofort Stummheit bedeutet, ein Bild des…….) Und nun sucht man, infolge einer Überlegung vielleicht die Augen. Alle diese flachen, seitlich hingelegten, wie mit Uhrgläsern überdeckten Augen, an die die im Wasser schwimmenden Bilder herangetrieben sind, solange sie schauten. Nicht anders waren sie damals, ebenso blicklos gleichgültig: denn Blicke trüge das Wasser nicht. Ebenso seicht und untief, leer herausgewendet, wie Wagenlaternen bei Tag. Aber hingetragen durch Widerstand und Bewegung jener dichteren Welt, warfen sie, leicht und sicher, Zeichnung um Zeichnung, Wink und Wendung, einwärts in ein uns unbekanntes Bewußtsein. Still und sicher trieben sie her, vor dem glatten Entschluß, ohne ihn zu verraten; still und sicher standen sie tagelang der Strömung entgegen, überzogen von ihr, von Schattenfluchten verdunkelt. Nun aber sind sie ausgelöst aus den langen Strähnen ihres Schauens, flach hingelegt, ohne daß es deshalb möglich ware, in sie einzudringen. Die Pupille wie mit schwarzem Stoff bezogen, der Umkreis um sie aufgelegt, wie dünnstes Blattgold. Mit einem Schrecken, ähnlich dem, den man beim Beißen auf etwas Hartes erfährt, entdeckt man die Undurchdringlichkeit dieser Augen—, und plötzlich meint man, vor lauter Stein und Metall zu stehen, wie man über Tisch hinsieht. Alles Gebogene ist hart anzusehen, und der Haufen stahlglänzender, pfriemenförmiger Fische, liegt kalt und schwer wie Haufen Werkzeuge da, mit denen andere, die das Aussehn von Steinen haben, geschliffen worden sind. Denn da nebenan liegen sie: runde glatte Achate, von braunen, blassen und goldenen Adern durchzogen, Streifen von rötlich-weißem Marmor, Jadestücke von vorsichtig gewölbtem Schliff, teilweise bearbeitete Topase, Bergkristall

The Fishmongers' Showcase

They lie in groups on a slight, gracious marble counter, some on the damp stone with a bit of blackish moss laid under, others in shallow chip baskets that had become dark from the moisture. Under there is one that is silver scaled, bent around on top, like a sword hand on a coat of arms, so that the silver spins and shimmers. On top of it, silver scaled, laying cross-wise, as if made of old silver, tarnished black, jaws jutting out, there's one that is horrifying, as it seems to come right out of the pile behind it. One first had noticed something with jaws, so one looks, there and over there, still another, and another, flops about in lamentation. (I might mention that what one calls "lamentation" arises happily, because here the figure that arises as voiced immediately signifies muteness, a picture of which......) And now, perhaps because of a reflection, one looks at the eyes. These are all flat, laid on their side, as if the eyes were covered by watchface bezels, but while they stared, images of swimming in water floated in them. Back then, they were no different, just as apathetically sightless: because the eyes would not take the weight of the water. Just as shallow, lacking depth, vacantly turned outwards, like a wagon's lamp during the day. But, carrying the dense world through every resistance, and in each of it's movements, they were cast inwards, light and sure, pattern around pattern, hint and turn, in an awareness we cannot fathom. They are driven in this silently and surely, with smooth resolve, without betraying themselves; they stood silently and surely for days against the current, overrun by it, dulled by the flow of shadows. But now they are released from the long strands of their stares, laid flat, it not being possible for them to be otherwise, to force our way into them. The pupils are covered with black material, the uvea float up around them, like gold leaf. With a terror, like one suffers having bitten down on something hard, one discovers the impenetrability of these eyes—, and suddenly one thinks he stands before nothing but stone and metal, as if one is looking at a table. Every curve looks hard, and the more dazzling steel-colored pile, the awl-shaped fish, lay cold and heavy, like a pile of tools, with differences among them as with stones that have been polished. They lie there, then, as if next door: smooth, round agates, shot through with brown, pale and golden veins, striped ones of red-white marble, carefully cut, bulbous jade pieces, partly processed topaz, crystals with sharp amethysts, opals from jellyfish. And an extremely thin layer

mit Spitzen von Amethyst, Opale aus Quallen. Und eine ganz dünne Schicht verweilenden Wassers ist noch über ihnen allen und trennt sie von diesem Licht, in dem sie fremd sind, verschlossen Behälter, die man vergebens zu öffnen versucht hat.

(Neapel 1906)
(trägt, im Taschenbuch, den Vermerk: "um es einmal zu machen.")

of water still remains over them all and separates them from this light, in which they are strange, sealed off, a container that one has tried to open in vain.

(Naples, 1906)
(found, in the notebook, with the remark:"do something with this one day.")

Wir sind nur Mund. Wer singt das ferne Herz,
das heil inmitten aller Dinge weilt?
Sein großer Schlag ist in uns eingeteilt
in kleine Schläge. Und sein großer Schmerz
ist, wie sein großer Jubel, uns zu groß.
So reißen wir uns immer wieder los
und sind nur Mund. Aber auf einmal bricht
der große Herzschlag heimlich in uns ein,
so daß wir schrein—,
und sind dann Wesen, Wandlung und Gesicht.

(Schöneck, 1922)

We are just voice. Who sings the remote heart
that remains unbroken 'midst all *things*?
Its stronger beat divides into tiny beats
in us. And its greater pain
is, like its greater joy, too large for us.
So, ever again, we tear ourselves loose
and are just voice. But suddenly the strong
heartbeat strikes once, secretly in us,
so that we shriek—,
and are then essence, change and face.

(Schöneck, 1922)

Die Frucht

Das stieg zu ihr aus Erde, stieg und stieg,
und war verschwiegen in dem stillen Stamme
und wurde in der klaren Blüte Flamme,
bis es sich wiederum verschwieg.

Und fruchtete durch eines Sommers Länge
in dem bei Nacht und Tag bemühten Baum,
und kannte sich als kommendes Gedränge
wider den teilnahmsvollen Raum.

Und wenn es jetzt im rundenden Ovale
mit seiner vollgewordnen Ruhe prunkt,
stürzt es, verzichtend, innen in der Schale
zurück in seinen Mittelpunkt.

(Muzot, Anfang 1924)

Fruit

It climbed there towards you out of the earth, it climbed
and climbed and what was withdrawn in its quiet roots
was transformed in the flames of its clear blossoms
until it hid itself again.

And ripened through a long summer
in which the tree struggled night and day
and knew itself to be coming together in a crush
in opposition to the sympathetic affordances about it.

And when it now is a resplendent rounded
oval with its fully formed quiet,
it falls, sacrificing, inwardly, in its soul
deep in its core.

(Muzot, Early 1924)

Das Füllhorn

(geschrieben für Hugo von Hofmannsthal)

Schwung und Form des gebendsten Gefäßes,
an der Göttin Schulter angelehnt;
unsrer Fassung immer ungemäßes,
doch von unserm Sehnen ausgedehnt—:

In der Tiefe seiner Windung faßt es
aller Reife die Gestalt und Wucht,
und das Herz des allerreinsten Gastes
wäre Form dem Ausguß solcher Frucht.

Obenauf der Blüten leichte Schenkung,
noch von ihrer ersten Frühe kühl,
alle kaum beweisbar, wie Erdenkung,
und vorhanden, wie Gefühl…

Soll die Göttin ihren Vorrat schütten
auf die Herzen, die er überfüllt,
auf die vielen Häuser, auf die Hütten,
auf die Wege, wo das Wandern gült?

Nein, sie steht in Überlebensgröße,
hoch, mit ihrem Horn voll Übermaß.
Nur das Wasser unten geht, als flöße
es ihr Geben in Gewächs und Gras.

(Februar 1924; Muzot)

The Cornucopia

(written for Hugo von Hofmannsthal)

Sweep and shape of the offering vessel
laid on the goddess' shoulder;
our composure is always lost,
yet from the stretched torsion of our tendons—;

In the depths of its coil, it holds
all ripening of form and power,
and the heart of the well-ordered guests
would be the shape for the spout of such fruit.

On top of the effortless gift of flowers,
still cool from their first dawn,
everything is barely limned, as on a blueprint
and close at hand, like a feeling…

If the goddess were to pour her stores
on our hearts, overflowing them,
on the old houses, on the huts,
on the roads, where would the wanderer still be valid?

No, she stands larger than life,
tall, with her full horn of plenty.
It's only the water that falls, as if to
shed her gifts on the herbs and grass.

(February 1924—Muzot)

Irrlichter

Wir haben einen alten Verkehr
mit den Lichtern in Moor.
Sie kommen mir wie Großtanten vor…
Ich entdecke mehr und mehr

zwischen ihnen und mir den Familienzug,
den keine Gewalt unterdrückt:
diesen Schwung, diesen Sprung, diesen Ruck, diesen Bug,
an den andern nicht glückt.

Auch ich bin dort, wo die Wege nicht gehn
im Schwaden, den mancher mied,
und ich habe mich oft verlöschen sehn
unter dem Augenlid.

(Februar 1924; Muzot)

Will-o-the-Wisps

We have an old bit of trade
with the lights on the moors.
They come towards me like great-aunts…
I spot more and more

among them, a procession of families
which no force can suppress:
the swings, the leaps, the tugs, the bows,
which don't affect the others.

I am there too, where the roads don't go,
in the swales which some avoid,
and I often have seen myself fading away
under my eyelids.

(February, 1924—Muzot)

Da dich das geflügelte Entzücken
über manchen frühen Abgrund trug,
baue jetzt der unerhörten Brücken
kühn berechenbaren Bug.

Wunder ist nicht nur im unerklärten
Überstehen der Gefahr;
erst in einer klaren reingewährten
Leistung wird das Wunder wunderbar.

Mitzuwirken, ist nicht Überhebung
an dem unbeschreiblichen Bezug,
immer inniger wird die Verwebung,
nur Getragensein ist nicht genug.

Deine ausgeübten Kräfte spanne,
das sie reichen zwischen zwein
Widersprüchen… Denn im Manne
will der Gott beraten sein.

(Februar 1924; Muzot)

Winged joy took you there
over many young chasms,
now it boldly builds the measured spans
of the incredible bridge.

The wonder is not just in the unresolved
persistence of the danger;
from the first, the achievement, in its clear, absolute-
givenness, makes the wonder miraculous.

To be worked-in is not something that can be
assumed for the inexpressible referent;
the weave is ever more intimate,
to be worn is not enough.

May the powers you exert span out
until they connect two
opposing views… then God
will be discussed among men.

(February, 1924—Muzot)

Vorfrühling

Härte schwand. Auf einmal legt sich Schonung
an der Wiesen aufgedecktes Grau.
Kleine Wasser ändern die Betonung.
Zärtlichkeiten, ungenau,

greifen nach der Erde aus dem Raum.
Wege gehen weit ins Land und zeigens.
Unvermutet siehst du seines Steigens
Ausdruck in dem leeren Baum.

(Muzot, März/April ?1924)

Early Spring

Harshness fades. Suddenly such mercy is laid
on the grays of the exposed meadows.
No water alters the accent.
Sweet nothings, vaguely

fumble at the earth from the affordances.
Roads go off into the countryside to point at it.
Unexpectedly, you see the expression
of its appearance in the empty trees.

(Muzot, March/April ? 1924)

Flugsand der Stunden. Leise fortwährende Schwindung
auch noch des glücklich gesegneten Baus.
Leben weht immer; schon ragen ohne Verbindung
die nicht mehr tragenden Säulen heraus.

Aber Verfall: ist er trauriger als der Fontäne
Rückkehr zum Spiegel, den sie mit Schimmer bestaubt?
Halten wir uns dem Wandel zwischen die Zähne,
daß er uns völlig begreift in sein schauendes Haupt.

(1924; Muzot)

Flowing sands of the hours. Quiet the likewise
constant settling of the happily blessed house-frame.
Life always wends; already, the no-longer weight-bearing
column towers up without support.

But decay: isn't it sadder than the fountain's
reappearance in a mirror, which it dusts with a shimmer?
We clamp change between our teeth
so that, in its surveying head, it fully comprehends us.

(1924—Muzot)

Ach, wie ihr heimlich vergeht!
Wer hat es verstanden,
daß ihr Nachen gedreht
ohne zu landen?

Keiner erfaßt es. Wo singt
rühmend ein Mund?
Alles vertaucht und ertrinkt,
drängt sich am Grund.

Drüberhin treibt uns der Schwung,
wie das Gefäll ihn leiht…
Nichtmal zur Spiegelung
bleibt uns Zeit.

(Anfang 1924; Muzot)

O, how you all secretly vanish!
Who has understood
that you might have steered towards the night
with no intention to land.

No one gets it. Where is there a voice
that sings with praises?
Everything sinks away and drowns,
piling up on the seabed.

For us, the swing pushes aloft,
what the drop lent it…
For us, time never stays
in the mirror.

(Early 1924; Muzot)

Götter schreiten vielleicht immer im gleichen Gewähren
  wo unser Himmel beginnt;
wie in Gedanken erreicht unsere schwereren Ähren,
  sanft sie wendend ihr Wind.

Wer sie zu fühlen vergaß, leistet nicht ganz die Verzichtung:
  dennoch haben sie teil.
Schweigsam, einfach und heil legt sich an seine Errichtung
  plötzlich ihr anderes Maß.

(1924; Muzot)

Perhaps the gods always walk in the same confidence
        that the sky starts in us;
but how our heavier heads are caught up in thought,
        gently turning in their wind.

Anyone who forgot to feel, fails to entirely complete the sacrifice:
        nevertheless they have a share.
Reserved, straight-forward and intact, he is arranged on his scaffold
        whose measure is suddenly different.

(1924; Muzot)

Spaziergang

Schon ist mein Blick am Hügel, dem besonnten
dem Wege, den ich kaum begann, voran.
So faßt uns das, was wir nicht fassen konnten,
voller Erscheinung aus der Ferne an—

und wandelt uns, auch wenn wirs nicht erreichen,
in jenes, das wir, kaum es ahnend, sind;
ein Zeichen weht, erwidernd unserm Zeichen…
Wir aber spüren nur den Gegenwind.

(Anfang 1924; Muzot)

A Walk

I look carefully at the hill, there in the sun,
at the path in front of me that I've scarcely begun.
From the far-off, a rife appearance, which we can't
grab hold of, touches us.

and it changes us, even if we don't reach each
place we see, since we scarcely can foresee where we'll be;
a sigil waves about, in answer to our signal...
but we just feel the wind in our faces.

(Early 1924; Muzot)

Schon kehrt der Saft aus jener Allgemeinheit,
die dunkel in den Wurzeln sich erneut,
zurück ans Licht und speist die grüne Reinheit,
die unter Rinden noch die Winde scheut.

Die Innenseite der Natur belebt sich,
verheimlichend ein neues Freut-Euch;
und eines ganzen Jahres Jugend hebt sich,
unkenntlich noch, ins starrende Gesträuch.

Des alten Nußbaums rühmliche Gestaltung
füllt sich mit Zukunft, außen grau und kühl;
doch junges Buschwerk zittert vor Verhaltung
unter der kleinen Vögel Vorgefühl.

(Frühling 1924; Muzot)

Already, the sap is churned out of that common good
which, dark in its roots, renews itself,
comes back into the light, and feeds on the green purity
hidden from the winds under the bark.

The inner surface of nature comes to life,
hiding a new "if you please;"
and an entire year's youth rises,
still unrecognizable, in the stark thickets.

The praiseworthy shape of the old walnuts,
outwardly grey and cool, fills with future;
and yet the young bushes tremble with restraint
in anticipation of the tiny birds.

(Spring, 1924; Muzot)

....
Wie sich die gestern noch stummen
Räume der Erde vertonen;
nun voller Singen und Summen:
Rufen und Antwort will wohnen.
......

(1924)

....
How the spaces of the earth that
yesterday were still mute resound;
Now, fuller songs and humming:
calls and answers want life.

......

(1924)

Wasser berauschen das Land.
Ein atemlos trinkender Frühling
taumelt geblendet ins Grün
und stößt seiner Trunkenheit Atem
aus den Münden der Blust.

Tagsüber üben die Nachtigalln
ihres Fühlens Entzückung
und ihre Übermacht
über den nüchternen Stern.

(Frühling 1924; Muzot)

Waters intoxicate the land.
A breathlessly more thirsty Spring
staggers, dazzled in the green
and pushes its drunken breath
from the mouths of blossoms.

During the day, the nightingale practices
the rapture of its feelings
and its superiority
over the sober stars.

(Spring 1924; Muzot)

Quellen, sie münden herauf,
beinah zu eilig.
Was triebt aus Gründen herauf
heiter und heilig?

Läßt dort im Edelstein
Glanz sich bereiten,
um uns am Wiesenrain
schlicht zu begleiten.

Wir, was erwidern wir
solcher Gebärde?
Ach, wie zergliedern wir
Wasser und Erde!

(1924)

Springs, that well up here
almost too quickly.
How do you push up, bright and
holy, from the ground?

There, in the brilliance of
precious stones, may you artlessly
prepare to be our companions
at the meadow's edge.

What could we say to
such a gesture?
Alas, how we parse
water and earth!

(1924)

Da schwang die Schaukel durch den Schmerz—, doch siehe,
der Schatten wars des Baums, an dem sie hängt.

Ob ich nun vorwärtsschwinge oder fliehe,
vom Schwunge in den Gegenschwung gedrängt,
das alles ist noch nicht einmal der Baum.
Mag ich nun steiler schwingen oder schräger,
ich fühle nur die Schaukel; meinen Träger
gewahr ich kaum.

So laß uns herrlich einen Baum vermuten,
der sich aus Riesenwurzeln aufwärtsstammt,
durch den unendlich Wind und Vögel fluten
und unter dem, in reinen Hirtenamt,
die Hirten sannen und die Herden ruhten.

Und daß durch ihn die starken Sterne blitzen,
macht ihn zur Maske einer ganzen Nacht.
Wer reicht aus ihm bis zu den Göttersitzen,
da uns sein Wesen schon nachdenklich macht?

(1923 die ersten zwei Zeilen, 1924 der Rest)

Thus, the swing swang through the pain—, but look
the shadow belongs to the tree on which it was caught.

Whether I swing forwards or flee,
propelled by momentum in an opposite arc,
none of this is even remotely the tree.
Were I to swing more steeply or at a slant,
I'd just feel the swing; I barely touch
the saddle.

So, may we delightfully imagine a tree,
one that draws itself up from its filtering roots
through the endless wind and floods of birds,
and beneath which, in a pure pasture,
herdsmen muse and the flocks rest.

And, make it a mask for the entire night,
so that the thick stars flash through it.
Is what stretches from it to the seat of the gods
what makes us really wonder about its essence?

(The first two lines, 1923; the rest, 1924)

Noch fast gleichgültig ist dieses Mit-dir-sein…
doch über ein Jahr schon, Erwachsenere, kann es vielleicht dem Einen,
der dich gewahrt, unendlich bedeuten:
Mit dir sein!

Ist Zeit nichts? Auf einmal kommt doch durch sie
dein Wunder. Daß diese Arme,
gestern dir selber fast lästig, einem,
den du nicht kennst, plötzlich Heimat
versprechen, die er nicht kannte. Heimat und Zukunft.

Daß er zu ihnen, wie nach Sankt-Jago di Compostella,
den härtesten Weg gehen will, lange,
alles verlassend. Daß ihn die Richtung
zu dir ergreift. Allein schon die Richtung
scheint ihm das Meiste. Er wagt kaum,
jemals ein Herz zu enthalten, das ankommt.

Gewölbter auf einmal, verdrängt deine heitere Brust
ein wenig mehr Mailuft: dies wird sein Atem sein,
dieses Verdrängte, das nach dir duftet.

(Juni 1924; Muzot)

This being-with-you is still almost an offhand thing…
yet perhaps for someone who stays with you over a year,
for an adult—it could seem endless:
to be with you!

Is time nothing? Nevertheless, suddenly your miracle
occurs in terms of it. These poor people,
almost tiresome to you yesterday,
whom you don't know, suddenly promised a
home, which you didn't know. Home and a future.

He wants to go to them, as if to Santiago de Compostela,
by the most difficult path, forsaking all
for a long time. This route took him
to you. Only the route already
seemed too heavy to him. He scarcely dared
to ever entertain the heart that arrives.

Even more concave suddenly, your serene breast expels
a little more of the May air: this will be what he breaths,
what's been expelled, what smells of you.

(June 1924; Muzot)

An der sonngewohnten Straße, in dem
hohlen halben Baumstamm, der seit lange
Trog ward, eine Oberfläche Wasser
in sich leis erneuernd, still ich meinen
Durst: des Wassers Heiterkeit und Herkunft
in mich nehmend durch die Handgelenke.
Trinken schiene mir zu viel, zu deutlich;
aber diese wartende Gebärde
holt mir helles Wasser ins Bewußtsein.

Also, kämst du, braucht ich, mich zu stillen,
nu rein leichtes Anruhn meiner Hände,
sei's an deiner Schulter junge Rundung,
sei es an den Andrang deiner Brüste.

(Juni 1924)

In the sun-dwelt street, in a
hollow halved tree trunk that had long since
become a trough, is a watery surface
in which, softly reviving, I quiet my
thirst; taking in the water's mirth and
origin through my wrists.
To drink seemed too much to me, too matter-of-fact;
but this expectant gesture
held me in the awareness of the bright water.

Were you to come like this, if I needed just a
light touch of my hand to quiet myself,
might it be on the youthful curve of your shoulder,
on the forward swell of your breast.

(June 1924)

Mädchen ordnen dem lockigen
Gott seinen Rebenhang;
Ziegen stocken, die bockigen
Weinbergmauern entlang.

Amsel formt ihren Lock-Ruf rund,
daß er rollt in den Raum;
Glück der Wiesen wird Hintergrund
für den glücklichen Baum.

Wasser verbinden, was abgetrennt
drängt ins verständigte Sein,
mischen in alles ein Element
flüssigen Himmels hinein.

(Juni 1924)

Girls clean their vined slopes;
for the curly-haired god,
goats balk, are stubborn,
along the vineyard moors.

A blackbird shapes its mellow caw-coo
he scrolls it out into the affordance;
the joy of the meadows becomes backdrop
for a joyful tree.

The waters that had separately pressed
forth in coherent Being rush together,
they mix an element of the
fluid skies into all things.

(June 1924)

Heißes Geschenk von den kältern
Bergen / versucht in den Juni den Sprung:
blinkend in Bach und Behältern
drängt sich Erneuerung.

Überall unter verstaubten
Büschen / lebendiger Wasser Gang;
und wie sie selig behaupten
Gehn sei Gesang.

(1924; Muzot)

A bright gift from the cold
mountains / tempts a leap in June:
gleaming in brook and pool,
renewal crowds forward.

Everywhere under the dusty
bushes / the more lively rush of waters;
and as they blissfully hold forth,
they go in song.

(1924; Muzot)

Durch den sich Vögel werfen, ist nicht der
vertraute Raum, der die Gestalt dir steigert.
(Im Freien, dorten, bist du dir verweigert
und schwindest weiter ohne Wiederkehr.)

Raum greift aus uns und übersetzt die Dinge:
daß dir das Dasein eines Baums gelinge,
wirf Innenraum um ihn, aus jenem Raum,
der in dir west. Umgib ihn mit Verhaltung.
Er grenzt sich nicht. Erst in der Eingestaltung
in dein Verzichten wird er wirklich Baum.

(Juni 1924; Muzot)

What birds drop through is not the
intimate affordance that intensifies form for you.
(There, in the Free you would refuse yourself
and dwindle away and never return.)

Affordance reaches from us and translates Things:
in order that the tree's being-there for you is accomplished,
throw inner-affordance about it, from that pure affordance
that's in you. Surround it with restraint.
It has no way to stop itself. Until in the in-forming
of your sacrifice it becomes an actual tree.

(June, 1924; Muzot)

Weißt du noch: fallende Sterne, die
quer wie Pferde durch die Himmel sprangen
über plötzlich hingehaltne Stangen
unsrer Wünsche—hatten wir so viele?—
den es sprangen Sterne, ungezählt;
fast ein jeder Aufblick war vermählt
mit dem raschen Wagnis ihrer Spiele,
und das Herz empfand sich als ein Ganzes
unter diesen Trümmern ihres Glanzes
und war heil, als überstünd es sie!

(1 Juni, Chorin-La-Chäpelle, 1924)

You still know: falling stars, which
leapt through the sky crosswise like horses
over the suddenly extended rods
of our wishes—have we so many?—
because countless stars leapt;
almost every look was married
to the rash hazards of their play,
and the heart felt itself to be whole
under the wreckage of their splendors
and was unhurt, as if it had weathered these.

(June 1ˢᵗ, Chorin-La-Chapelle, 1924)

Neigung: wahrhaftes Wort! Daß wir jede empfänden,
nicht nur die neuste, die uns ein Herz noch verschweigt:
wo sich ein Hügel langsam, mit sanften Geländen
zu der empfänglichen Wiese neigt,
sei es nicht weniger *unser*, sie uns vermehrlich;
oder des Vogels reichlicher Flug
schenke uns Herzraum, mache uns Zukunft entbehrlich.
Alles ist Überfluß. Denn genug
war es schon damals, als uns die Kindheit bestürzte
mit unendlichem Dasein. Damals schon
was es zuviel. Wie könnten wir jemals Verkürzte
oder Betrogene sein: wir mit jeglichem Lohn
längst Überlohnten....
....

(1922?)

124

Inclination: true word! That we *each* would find,
not just the newest, but that which still conceals a heart for us:
where there's a gradual rise, with gentle swales that
slope up to receptive meadows,
may it be no less ours, may it increase for us,
or may the purer flight of a bird
release a heart's affordance for us, may it make our future unnecessary.
All is overflow. Because even then
it was enough—when childhood confused us
with unending Being-Here. Even then
it was too much. As if we could ever be reduced
or deprived: with every payment we
are overpaid…
……….

(1922?)

…Wann wird, wann wird, wann wird es genügen
das Kagen und Sagen? Waren nicht Meister im Fügen
menschlicher Worte gekommen? Warum die neuen Versuche?

Sind nicht, sind nicht, sind nicht vom Buche
die Menschen geschlagen wie von fortwährender Glocke?
Wenn dir, zwischen zwei Büchern, schweigender Himmel erschient:

frohlocke…

oder ein Ausschnitt einfacher Erde im Abend.

Mehr als die Stürme, mehr als die Meere haben
die Menschen geschrieen… Welche Übergewichte von Stille
müssen im Weltraum wohnen, da uns die Grille
hörbar blieb, uns schreienden Menschen. Da uns die Sterne
schweigende scheinen, im angeschrieenen Äther!

Redeten uns die fernsten, die alten und ältesten Väter!
Und wir: Hörende endlich! Die ersten hörenden Menschen.

(Am Vorabend der Orpheus-Sonette geschrieben)

…when will, when will, when will lamentation and
speech be enough? Hasn't the master come
in the fugues of human words? What's with these new trials?

Aren't they, aren't they, aren't they from the book
that strikes men like an incessant bell?
If, between two books, the more silent sky appears to you: rejoice…
or a detail of the simple earth in the evening.

More than the storms, more than the seas, have
people cried… some preponderance of silence
must dwell in the affordances of the world, where the cricket
remains audible to us, to we crying people. There the stars shine
silently for us, in the air at which we cry!

The most distant, the ancient and oldest fathers spoke to us!
And we: hearers at last! The first people who hear.

(From the evening before the Orpheus Sonnets were written)

Idol

Gott oder Götter des Katzenschlafs,
kostende Gottheit, die in dem dunkeln
Mund reife Augen-Beeren zerdrückt,
süßgewordenen Schauns Traubensaft,
ewiges Licht in der Krypta des Gaumens.
Schlaf-Lied nicht,—Gong! Gong!
Was die anderen Götter beschwört,
entläßt diesen verlisteten Gott
an seine einwärts fallende Macht.

(November 1925)

Idol

God or goddess of the catnap,
costly deity, in whose dark
mouth ripe Eye-berries are crushed,
the grape juice of glances that were sweet,
that is eternal light in the palate's crypt.
Not a lullaby,—Gong! Gong!
What conjures forth the other gods
releases this mis-listed God
into his inwardly withdrawing power.

(November 1925)

Vasen-Bild
(Totenmahl)

Sieh, wie unsre Schalen sich durchdringen
ohne Klirrn. Und Wein geht durch den Wein
wie der Mond durch seinen Widerschein
im Gewölk. Oh stilles Weltverbringen...
Und der leichte Nicht-Klang spielt wie ein
Schmetterling mit andern Schmetterlingen,
welche tanzen um den warmen Stein.

Blinder Bissen wölbt sich ohne Gröbe
doch, genährt mit nichts wie die Amöbe
ließt ich, auch wenn ich näher höbe,
jenen Abstand dauern von vorhin;
und das einzige, das mich selbst verschöbe
ist der Schritt der Tänzerin.

(1922)

Image on a Vase
(Meal for the Dead)

See, how they pass through our skin
without clattering. And wine goes through wine
like the moon through its reflection
in the clouds. Oh, the silent ones who endure the world...
And a faint nothing-song plays like a
butterfly among other butterflies,
dancing a bit around the warm stones.

Blindly, a mouthful bulges though empty of anything
coarse, I let it feed on nothing like an
amoeba, even were I to draw it closer,
the gap between us would stay the same;
and the only thing which I would have delayed
is the dancers' step.

(1922)

Gong

Nicht mehr für Ohren…: Klang,
der, wie ein tieferes Ohr,
uns scheinbar Hörende, hört.
Umkehr der Räume. Entwurf
innerer Welten im Frein…
Tempel vor ihrer Geburt,
Lösung, gesättigt mit schwer
löslichen Göttern…: *Gong!*

Summe des Schweigenden, das
sich zu sich selber bekennt,
brausende Einkehr in sich
dessen, das an sich verstummt,
Dauer, aus Ablauf gepreßt,
um-gegossener Stern…: *Gong!*

Du, die man niemals vergißt,
die sich gebar im Verlust,
nichtmehr begriffenes Fest,
Wein an unsichtbarem Mund,
Sturm in der Säule, die trägt,
Wanderers Sturz in den Weg,
unser, an Alles, Verrat…: *Gong!*

Gong

Not for the ears any longer…: a clang
that, like a deeper ear that,
as if listening, hears us.
Echo of the Affordances. Blueprint of
more inward worlds in the free…
Temple of its birth,
solution, saturated by the heavy
soluble gods…: *Gong!*

Sum of the silences that confess,
one to the other, each
ringing a stop in itself
for the other, that itself goes silent,
duration, forced from the process,
star poured out into everything…: *Gong!*

You, whom one never forgets,
who give birth to yourself in loss,
no longer a festival in progress,
wine for an invisible mouth,
storm in the soul, that keeps on,
plunge of the wanderers on their way,
our betrayal of everything… *Gong!*

(1925)

Vollmacht

Ach entzögen wir uns / Zählern und Studenschlägern.
Einen Morgen hinaus / heißes Jungsein mit Jägern,
      Rufen im Hundegekläff.
Daß in durchdrängten Gebüsch / Kühle uns fröhlich besprühe,
und wir im Neuen und Frein / in en Lüften der Frühe
      fühlten den graden Betreff!

Solches war uns bestimmt. / Leichte beschwingte Erscheinung.
Nicht, im starren Gelaß, / nach einer Nacht voll Verneinung,
      ein verneinender Tag.
Diese sind ewig in Recht: / dringend dem Leben Genahte;
weil sie Lebendige sind, / tritt das unendlich bejahte
      Tier in den tödlichen Schlag.

Warrant

Alas, we seclude ourselves / in prayer and marking the hours.
One morning out / a burning youth with hunters, and
      calls among the yapping of the hounds.
There, in the bushes through which we passed, a coolness merrily spattered us
and, in the newness and freedom / in the morning breezes, we
      felt the assessing regard!

That's the way we were determined. / Slight, vibrant figures.
Not, in a tight dungeon, / after a night full of denial,
      on a day more denied.
This is an eternal law: / urgently approach life;
because they are alive, / the endlessly affirmed
      creature steps into the mortal blow.

Ankunft

In einer Rose steht dein Bett, Geliebte. Dich selber
(oh ich Schwimmer wider die Strömung des Dufts)
hab ich verloren. So wie dem Leben zuvor
diese (von außen nicht meßbar) dreimal drei Monate sind,
so nach innen geschlagen, werd ich erst *sein*. Auf einmal,
zwei Jahrtausende vor jenem neuen Geschöpf,
das wir genießen, wenn die Berührung beginnt,
plötzlich: gegen dir über, werd ich im Auge geboren.

Advent

Love, your bed stood in a rose. In you alone
(oh I swim against the drifting scents)
I was lost. As in the life before
this one (otherwise immeasurable) there were nine months,
so, after an inner struggle, I will *be* for the first time. All at once,
two thousand years with this new creature,
which we savor, when touch begins,
suddenly: facing you from above, I am being born in your eyes.

Gegen-Strophen

Oh, daß ihr hier, Frauen, einhergeht,
hier unter uns, leidvoll,
nicht geschonter als wir und dennoch imstande,
selig zu machen wie Selige.

Woher,
wenn der Geliebte erscheint,
nehmt ihr die Zukunft?
Mehr, als je sein wird.
Wer die Entfernungen weiß
bis zum äußersten Fixstern,
staunt, wenn er diesen gewahrt,
euern herrlichen Herzraum.
Wie, im Gedräng, spart ihr ihn aus?
Ihr, voll Quellen und Nacht.

Seid ihr wirklich die gleichen,
die, da ihr Kind wart,
unwirsch im Schulgang
anstieß der ältere Bruder?
Ihr Heilen.

     Wo wir als Kinder uns schon
     häßlich für immer verzerrn,
     wart ihr wie Brot vor der Wandlung.

Abbruch der Kindheit
war euch nicht Schaden. Auf einmal
standet ihr da, wie im Gott
plötzlich zum Wunder ergänzt.

Antistrophes

Oh, that you, Women, go about here,
here, among us, full of grief,
no more protected than we and nevertheless able
to act blissfully, like the Blessed.

How,
if a lover appears,
do you bear the future?
There's more than will ever be.
One who knows the distances
as far as the outermost fixed star,
is astonished when he becomes aware of
the magnificent affordance of your heart.
How, in the pushing crowd, do you spare it's being open?
You, wellspring and night.

Are you really the same
as the one—you were a child then—
an older brother bullied brusquely
on the way to school?
You are unmarred.

> When we as children were forever
> hideously contorted,
> you were like the bread before it's transformed.

The abrupt end of childhood
was not damaging for you. All at once
you stood there, like a God
suddenly replete in a miracle.

Wir, wie gebrochen vom Berg,
oft schon als Knaben scharf
an den Rändern, vielleicht
manchmal glücklich behaun;
wir, wie Stücke Gesteins,
über Blumen gestürzt.

Blumen des tieferen Erdreichs,
von allen Wurzeln geliebte,
ihr, der Eurydike Schwestern,
immer voll heiliger Umkehr
hinter dem steigenden Mann.

Wir, von uns selber gekränkt,
Kränkende gern und gern
Wiedergekränkte aus Not.
Wir, wie Waffen, dem Zorn
neben den Schlaf gelegt.

Ihr, die ihr beinah Schutz seid, wo niemand
schützt. Wie ein schattiger Schlafbaum
ist der Gedanke an euch
für die Schwärme des Einsamen.

(1914 und später)

We, as if broken off a mountain,
often, like a boy, sharp
at the edges, even if
sometimes fortunately cut;
we, like a lump of stone
that's fallen on a flower.

Flowers of deeper soil
loved by all roots,
you, sisters of Eurydice,
ever more saintly turned-back-one
behind the ascending man.

We alone have offended ourselves,
offended with pleasure and gladly
again offended by want.
We, who lay down to sleep with
our anger beside us like a weapon.

You, who are almost shelter enough for those whom
no one shelters. A thought of you is like
a shadier tree of sleep
for the swarms of the solitary.

(1914 and later)

Klage

Wem willst du klagen, Herz? Immer gemiedener
ringt sich dein Weg durch die unbegreiflichen
Menschen. Mehr noch vergebens vielleicht,
da er die Richtung behält,
Richtung zur Zukunft behält,
zu der verlorenen...

Früher, klagtest? Was wars? Eine gefallene
Beere des Jubels, unreife!
Jetzt aber bricht mir mein Jubelbaum,
bricht mir im Sturme mein langsamer
Jubel-Baum.
Schönster, in meiner unsichtbaren
Landschaft, der du mich kenntlicher
machtest Engeln, unsichtbaren.

(Paris, Anfang Juli 1914)

Lament

What will you lament, heart? Ever more shunned,
your path wrestles itself through the incomprehensible
people. Perhaps there is still more to forgive,
so the heart holds its course
holds its course into the future,
into the abandoned…

Did you lament before? About what? A fallen
bunch of the grapes of jubilation, unripe!
But now, my tree of jubilation comes to me
in the storm, my slower
Jubel-tree comes.
More beautiful, in my invisible
landscape, which you, Angel made
known to me, invisible.

(Paris, Early July, 1914)

Musik: Atem der Statuen, vielleicht:
Stille der Bilder. Du Sprache, wo Sprachen
enden; du Zeit,
die senkrecht steht auf der Richtung vergehender Herzen.
Gefühle, zu wem? Oh du, der Gefühle
Wandlung…, in was? In hörbare Landschaft.
Du Fremde, Musik. Du uns entwachsener
Herzraum. Innigstes unser, das uns übersteigend,
hinausdrängt…, heiliger Abschied:
da uns das Innre umsteht,
als geübteste Ferne, als andre
Seite der Luft,
rein,
riesig,
nicht mehr bewohnbar.

(1915, vermutlich, aus dem Besitz der Frau H.W.)

Music: breath of statues, perhaps:
Silence of images. You are speech, when speech
ends; you are time,
that stands perpendicular to the path of the transient heart.

Feelings, for whom? Oh you feelings of
transformation…, in what? In the audible landscape.
You are a stranger, music. You, the heart's affordance that
springs open in us. Our innermost, that wells up over us
pressing us out…., holier parting:
there the inner surrounds us,
as the most practiced distance, as a different
side of the air,
pure,
grand,
no longer habitable.

*(Written in the Guestbook of Frau Hanna Wolf
and dated Jan 11, and 12, 1918.)*

Appendices

A Different Side of the Air: Rilke's Last Suite of Poems

As noted in the introduction, this arrangement reflects Rilke's awareness of his illness and likely death. In keeping with this, the voice throughout is more personal than Rilke permitted in previous published collections, the "I" less the persona of the heroic or dedicated artist, than that of an artist who has little left to hide. Of course, this is still a persona—Rilke was nothing if not aware of the performative dimensions of language—but the retrospective mood allows a new immediacy and frankness. That directness is reflected in the language of the poems—overall the choice of verbal root or noun is more restricted, the shifts and turns of thought more starkly painted. A few of the selected poems are fragmentary and gnomic, some would be simple pastoral paintings except that a strange pressure is admitted that reminds us we cannot be at home in such landscape. And, for the first time he offers us a few passes at imagining the depths of the sea. At the end, one is left with the impression that the sense of the occasional about the collection as a whole and the at-times stark difficulty of the poetry stages an attitude Rilke wished to convey—about his work (and about what work can do), and about our place in death and life.

It shouldn't surprise us to find Rilke working on these themes, and yet, Rilke's late German poetry is frequently dismissed as occasional or slight, as if the problems of composition and song had been resolved for all time in the *Elegies* and *Sonnets*. This collection tells us otherwise; it shows Rilke continuing to explore the limits of his imagery and language, offering us versions, reconsideration and new settings for many of the figures and concepts to which he had always turned—figures such as the tree lifted up against a landscape, the night sky and stars, the arc of a ball in a child's game or the dart and call of a bird, the dead, the face of the lover and the search for one's own face, or the celebration of a young girl who'd been a passing friend; and notions of world (*welt*) and affordance or room (*raum*) extant both within being here and as an exterior open towards which we turn, and always his consideration of a *thing* and its relationship to us.

Rilke makes the connections between this last collection of poems and both previous collections and unpublished material explicit in several ways, chief of which is his return to the themes of unpublished material from 1912-1915, his arrangement of the collection as a whole as a transformational figure, and his use of material from a long-lost 1906 Capri journal as the center-piece of the collection.

For those unfamiliar with Rilke's biography, it is useful to briefly reprise several highlights. In his early 20s (1887-1900), Rilke began to establish himself as a writer and art critic, largely within what would elsewhere be called Art Nouveau circles. During this time he had a significant three-year love affair with an older Russian emigrée, Lou Andreas-Salomé, a woman whom Nietzsche had asked to marry him some fifteen years earlier. By 1900, Rilke and Lou were estranged, and he subsequently married a young German sculptor, Clara Westhoff, and had a child with her in 1901. In 1902, Rilke left Clara and his daughter Ruth and moved to Paris, ostensibly to work on a monograph on Rodin. Rilke would live on and off in Paris until forced to emigrate to Germany at the beginning of World War I. During the Paris years, Rilke worked as Rodin's secretary, wrote for art journals, and then began to have success with his first published collections of poems. In 1907-8, he published a two-volume collection *New Poems* that represents the fruits of his initial engagement with Modernist notions of self and aesthetic object. That work, the ongoing collapse of his marriage with Clara, and his struggle to realize the ideal of an ascetic artist-saint left him in a creative and personal crisis that led to an extended search for call [?????] and a subsequent renewal of inspiration over the winter of 1911-12. At that time he began work on the poems that, in 1922, would be completed as the *Duino Elegies*.

The idea of the poet or artist's call had considerable power both for Rilke himself and for those surrounding the poet who sensed he might accomplish a great work. Although Rilke was a fairly harsh critic of Christianity, his notion of the call was phrased in theological and spiritual terms. His early major work, *The Book of Hours* (1899-1900), *Stories of God,* and *Images of Christ* develop a theology focused on the work of an artist's inspiration. The years of 1908-11, saw Rilke first attempting to win such inspiration, like Zarathustra, through will alone, and then increasingly admitting the *relational* dimensions of inspiration which required a mediating figure or image. In 1912, Rilke began to develop the conceit of the mediating angel, and the poems of 1912-1914 show Rilke working through the terms of this figure, work that would not end until the 1922 revision of self and angel in the non-dual terms of the poet-God, Orpheus. For Rilke, the early efforts to imagine God anew were *realized* in the *Elegies* and *Sonnets*, and these offer something like a revelation for our times.

How then does the material of Rilke's last collection reflect this creative mythology? First, it is important to see that the realization of a revelation does not bring the work of spirit or life to an end—rather it establishes a workable measure that will necessarily have to be reprised (ritually and in new, further revelation). At the very least—a bit like the Zen story of the man who chops wood before and after enlightenment—there is a turn to the quotidian that can at last be borne. Both the French poems of 1923-1925, and the last collection in German reflect this kind of turn—we don't find Rilke looking *past* the appearing world; instead the work of life involves the *relation* of thought and image to sense world and the play of this in art.

Second, Rilke identified several of the 1924 poems as belonging to the material for *Poems to the Night*. That title refers to an unpublished set of poems from 1912-13 that Rilke set down in a folio for his friend Rudolf Kassner; in 1916 Rilke sent a second copy of this to his publisher. His identification of later poems as belonging to this cycle suggest he still imagined the *Night* poems as a possible manuscript project and link the poems to both the problems he'd taken up in the *Night* poems and to the early moments of new inspiration in 1912 that these reflect.

Poems to the Night brought together poems written following the famous initial opening of the work on the *Elegies* in January 1912. This last is probably one of the best known events in Rilke's life—while staying alone at Duino Castle on the Adriatic Coast and having just completed revisions on the cycle, *Life of the Virgin Mary*, Rilke hears the first words of the *Duino Elegies*—"O, if I cried out, who, among the ranks of angels, would hear me"—as if spoken from the wind and, in just a day-and-a-half, has composed the bulk of the first two Elegies.

As noted above, the years 1909-1911 for Rilke had been marked by a search for radical inspiration. Over 1911, he had spent considerable time reading the poetry and imagining the lives of women poets who had found inspiration in unrequited love—he had worked on translations of the sonnets of Louise Labé and the then famous love letters of a Portuguese Nun, and in November 2011, worked on a translation of Dante's *Vita Nuova* with his friend and patron (and owner of Duino), the Princess Maria von Thurn und Taxis. The work on the manuscript for *Life of the Virgin Mary* brought him face to face with Mary's startling encounter with the Angel Gabriel—those first words that came to him out of the air realize the longing he'd been struggling with as a longing to be so elected.

Over the next two years, Rilke searched more actively for traces of an angel that might speak to him. In accordance with instructions imparted by an "Unknown Woman" as channeled at a séance by the Princess Maria's son, Rilke travelled to Spain the following winter (1913) in search of a spiritual encounter, and then, in July 1913, visited his muse and prior lover, Lou Andreas Salomé, for the first time in some eight years. The bulk of *Poems to the Night* were then written in Paris over the fall and early winter of 1913. And then all of this impetus would be torn apart the following autumn with the onset of World War I.

The relationship of *Poems to the Night* to the *Duino Elegies* is hardly casual. The poems critique the Romantic conceit that finds radical beauty in the imagined utter darkness of night and call for and imagine the existence of an inspiring angel and its consolations and severity. The image of the lover met in bed at night, the night sky that opens its face over the bed of one alone or waiting for a lover, and the angel that insists mingle and trade places in these poems, and all this argues against the dialectical conceit that the path of realization leads through radical absence or negation. These poems contradict the notion, extant since Novalis' *Hymns to the Night*, of the night (and death) as a radical absence whose fact confronts self. Instead, the night is full of stars and the half seen face of a lover on a pillow, is lit by the dim lights of town or the moon, and is never, anywhere, anything like a "not-being" that might soothe us.

By 1924, Rilke had seen that he had explored the relation of self-and-other through a variety of motifs—through an exploration of the interrelation of self and thing (*ding*), by a consideration of the relation of the living to the dead, as the product of a series of reciprocating movements (the throw of a ball back and forth between two children or the movements of a dancer)—and he had interrogated aesthetic expression as a movement in such a relation or dance (the tree lifted up against sky that is a leitmotif for the figure an artist brings into being by his hand or words or song). The completion of the *Sonnets to Orpheus* had presented him with the inescapability of these relations, and thus he no longer sought to be completed in relation to a *primary* figure (such as the Angel or the lover) or *topos*. In the 1926 volume, Rilke reprises the settings and gestures of the *Poems to the Night*, but the night itself is no longer a master figure he sets himself in relation to. Rather, the relationship of solitary person to night sky, as well as the relations posed by the stars and planets (either as astrological angles or as constellations of fixed stars) are offered as one *motif* among many for exploring and depicting the relation of self-and-other. And there is no citation of a mediating angel—what mediates now is the perspective offered by one or another setting, be it night sky or graveyard, moonlit garden or old, once-lost notebook.

For Rilke, the effort to trace out and describe the relation of self-and-other was less an epistemic of mapping, than an effort to realize a *transformation* that occurs to both self and other in their relation and, in particular, to accomplish or provide the relational basis for a transformation for an other that would become possible by the realization of an aesthetic image in a given medium. This meant that he began to imagine not only transformational actors like the poet-God Orpheus, but also that appearance itself, and thus, any aesthetic image also, could be conceived of as a site of transformational energies. In the *Sonnets to Orpheus*, he attempts to capture the transformational dynamics of the image of a recently deceased young women—elsewhere he had worked with the figure of a rose as a leitmotif for a figure that, impossibly, worked transformation in us.

The third way in which the 1926 collection reprises and restages Rilke's larger project is in the arrangement of the poems itself and the way in which this arrangement formally stages Rilke's ideas of transformational figuration. For Rilke, a transformational figure, such as the tree-dancer of Sonnet II.18, is not simply a union of opposites (self-and-other, life-and-death, girl-and-tree) but the impossible existence of both of these as such at the same time. This is clearest in what he says about the rose in a set of short French poems written in Sept. 1924; there he describes the rose not as a single thing or surface but as impossibly both a thing that exists in relation to unfathomable depths but also a thing that is itself opened out surface. What the rose *is*, is neither surface nor depth, neither appearance nor something like essence—rather the rose exists as a single thing that is *both* surface and depth, without either of these modes of being ever being reduced or equal to the other. For Rilke, a transformational figure is one that is undone even as it is realized (the glass that shatters as it rings) not because of any necessary reciprocal summation, but because in it is realized a double movement we cannot otherwise say.

How then does the arrangement of the 1926 volume produce a transformational figure—how is it something like the rose, or the dancer who is also tree, how is it like Orpheus who impossibly exists in both the realm of the living and the realm of the dead, and in doing so produces a figure of how thought and body might be woven so as to open out, rather than to confine? Rilke does this by arranging the texts of 1924 around material from a long-lost journal in a manner that both undoes the possibility of the text being any kind of whole (that works against its principles of arrangement) and yet nevertheless coheres as a design.

The basic structure of the book takes the poems of 1924 as its rough clay. The poems were written over the course of the year, and many are seasonally specific. Like day-and-night, and male-female, a year is one of our fundamental measures of what constitutes a "complete unit" or cycle—the sequence of the seasons is what Vendler, working with Dickinson's poems, calls a chromatic sequence, a movement that takes place over time (and out into a future) that nevertheless does not lose its way. One might imagine using the order or sequence of the seasons as a frame for organizing a set of occasional poems as a meaningful whole, and there are many, many books that do just this. Rilke's approach is different, and his choices are pertinent.

The collection can be roughly broken into three sections. The first includes poems from 1924 and a few from Rilke's last visit to Paris in the summer of 1925. This is followed by the material from the 1906 Capri journal, laid out as if in the order of the daybook. And finally we get a second sequence of poems roughly equal to the first. Approximately 2/3 of these are from 1924, but this third section ends with a set of ten poems dating again from 1925 but ending with poems from 1914-5. The seasonal is brought to bear on the whole because Rilke arranges the material from 1924 in the first and third sections against the grain of a "realistic" delineation of the seasons.

Rilke begins the collection as a whole with the poem 'Autumn,' and poems from the Fall and late Summer of 1924 make up the background for this section. If one looks at Rilke's published poetry, it is quite clear that the initial poem of a sequence is designed as an entrance or bookplate that frames the reader's experience of the whole. *The Book of Images* begins quite literally with a poem titled 'Entrance' that describes the poet wearily going to his doorway and using his eyes to draw a tree against the horizon, a gesture that is repeated in the *Sonnets to Orpheus* when in the first poem, Orpheus is described as lifting up a sheltering tree with his voice. 'Autumn' similarly begins, "Oh, higher tree in our glaze," but considers the tree against a background boundless sky that "breaks through its branches." Here, the framing background is, like the future season and like what Rilke elsewhere calls the open, a beyond-measure that faces any figure. It is, furthermore, a sky-beyond-measure that—given the biographical context—is more like death's-beyond which we do not yet know than the sky-beyond-measure that is spring. And it's an awkward poem, with a line drawn across the ending, so that its having been constructed as such is visible.

How then is the rest of the section composed? Rilke follows his initial poem with a series of short poems, several of which appear to be fragmentary, that date later than the initial poem. Three date from the following summer (1925), one from later in the fall. The first of the three is fragmentary but introduces an image—a balancing scale—that will become a key motif for this first section. The second is the short, exquisite 'O not to be separate'—one of the key passages in Rilke's work for the delineation of what he means by the "inner" dimension of self or thing. The third a rather awkward poem that reprises the opening of *The Book of Hours* by describing the poet as being on a ceaseless journey toward realization. Here, instead of circling around and around the tower—Rilke's perhaps prescient evocation of a search for call—the path leads out, away from a mother's lap into a beyond-which he cannot imagine. The last is the relatively well-known poem "Now is the time that the gods would step out / of the *things* they had inhabited…" that again speaks of a moving beyond, an out-into that would occur as a translucent interiority tore itself out of and into life.

Following these opening gestures, Rilke offers two set-pieces. The first is a fairly well-realized suite of three poems from 1925, 'O, Lacrimosa.' In this sequence, Rilke begins to weave tropes. He describes a weeping woman who is "the Balanced Scale of all tears," "who did not feel she was sky," whose "pain-land" comes into view like a face across from you in a bed, whose face is imagined to be "a balance against the world's depths." These motifs from *Poems to the Night* preface first a declaration that "emptiness is nothing but a breath" (i.e., that it is not nothing) and then the lament, "O Winter!" that seems to presage a still-forward movement from Autumn into the depths of the year and by this also presages how a year might turn.

The second set-piece is a suite of nine poems, all written in June 1924, all but one written during Rilke's stay at a spa in Ragaz. The suite, 'Nine Poems Written in a Churchyard in Ragaz' offer a miniaturized setting for the motifs Rilke is exploring. The churchyard is also a grave-yard, and we encounter the dead both externally in the quotidian silence of grave, flower, play of light, and butterfly and in the "interior" visualization of a ritual meal shared with the dead. The fifth poem and thus hinge of the sequence is center-justified rather than left-justified and offers a meditation on life and death through the figure of a balancing scale—thus in two ways Rilke signals some significance with respect to this image, some way in which the "middle" might matter. And the seventh is a three-part poem that reflects on a ball left by a child's grave, giving Rilke an opportunity to explore the movement of growth (the movement into the beyond-which of the new year, the movement of child away from mother) as a back-and-forth that is both the child's movement into life and death and the back-and-forth between the far into which one throws the ball and its return. The eighth poem picks up the context of the seventh but instead of the back-and-forth of a game of catch considers the play of hide-and-seek where the movement is between tree and center and where roles are traded so that we are at one time seeker and hider the next.

The sequence concludes with nine poems. These include two poems identified as belonging to *Poems to the Night*, two more set at night, and one that reprises the motif of drinking world from the face of the beloved found in *Poems to the Night*. The remaining four include the initial poem of this series, 'Magic,' which offers an *ars poetica* identifying language as doubled or two-sided (see discussion of this poem in the Notes), one that explores the dynamics by which things are brought into meaningful relation with each other, and two—'The Palm and the Hand' and 'Gravity' that stress a dynamic middle (*Mitte*) in the midst of what otherwise exchanges place. These last continue the meditation on the back-and-forth marked by the motif of the scale and of play, a back-and-forth that is both "magic," because impossibly involving two separate vectors and "miraculous," because impossible.

All of these last poems are from Fall 1924, so that in this initial set of poems, both the suggestion of a temporal sequence (a movement from Fall through winter to a subsequent year) and a single season are quoted. We venture out from the beginning as if into the open, and yet the weight of the poems belies that movement, extends a measure, and here, the return to the season from which we departed acts in consort with the motif of a center in the midst of transformation. And the sequence contains at least two set-piece "jewels," that are themselves sequences that combine movement and repose, but nevertheless develop what is, in the end, a play of images woven around lament that occurs both lyrically in the sway between lines and at the level of semantics.

Rilke's decision to place the material from the 1906 Capri journal at the center of the collection as a whole opens out further dimensions of this sensibility. This journal was among several boxes of personal papers Rilke had left behind in Paris in the rush to leave the city at the onset of the war in Sept 1914. He was told that all had been lost, but during his last stay in Paris over the late spring and summer of 1925, the journal and a few other papers were unearthed and returned to him. The writing in the journal thus has the status of a recovered memory, the pages giving him unexpected access to material from another time.

In terms of content, the poems in the Capri journal are some of the earliest to use the motif of wandering alone in the mountains as a trope for realizing Rilke's sense of being homeless in the world—he would reprise these notes in several unpublished poems written in the early days of his flight to Germany in the fall of 1914 and there are echoes of this in poems included in *Poems to the Night* such as 'Spanish Trilogy' and 'The Great Night.' In these poems Rilke begins to treat as his own a homelessness he had previously brooded over as characteristic of the poor—there is a shift from third person to first person that, in keeping with his modernist context, considers such alienation as a possibly universal condition.

In addition, the journal offered Rilke the then extent traces of days he would elsewhere mark as having had spiritual significance. In Spain in 1913, Rilke would compose a description of a reverie that occurred to him some weeks after his realization of the first two Elegies in January 1912. This description is included in his collected prose as 'Lived-Experience' (*Erlebnis*); it recounts an experience of what appears to be non-dual awareness that occurred to him when he leaned against an olive tree in a grove in the castle environs. In the account, he links that experience to a similar sense of non-dual being that occurred to him during the weeks at Capri in 1906 when he'd heard a bird call, a personal realization likely linked to the critical turn of the Seventh Elegy when, after having exhaustively considered human finitude in Elegies I-VI, Rilke realizes the terms of a nevertheless ecstatic opening in "a bird's call." Hence, for Rilke, the material from 1906 would be linked to his experience of an affective basis he would later reprise in his poetic answer to human finitude.

While Rilke does not directly cite an experience of equipoise as the middle of this collection, it's an odd coincidence that the poem from the Capri journal that falls at the rough middle of the collection as a whole is 'The Night of the Spring Equinox,' an occasional poem that follows Rilke's eye from a description of the play of shadows and light on the garden paths upward to "the great stars in the equinoctial night" that stand "strong and diamond-like" above the "weathered trees… in the deep, solemn in-between affordances (*Zwischenräumen*)." What this vertical gesture draws is what Celan might have called a meridian, or H.D., a herm—an edge, measure bar, the point in the game at which the ball begins to return, hurtling back towards us.

It would be one thing to say this answer—perhaps the angel's attention or God's—existed as a positive fact, immediate to us. And yet, it may be that language cannot do this or that, to speak of this truly, the saying has to be put off. And this "putting off" occurs because the poem is out of the time of the collection as a whole, even as it names a moment that occurs apparently within it. For, if the first set of poems establishes the Autumn of 1924 as the beginning of the sequence, then in terms of the cycle of the seasons we should come to the Spring Equinox of the following year, we should undergo the transformation that occurs at this moment of equipoise. And yet, the equinox cited is from long ago, so that in this sense it is covered or set out of the sequence, and citing it brings another time *to* the sequence. Suddenly time also is doubled—still and not, sense and memory mingled as being in time, and we are both where we are and not. And this occurs not with a trumpet's blast, but by a decision to cede space to the personal.

Did Rilke know in the spring of 1906 that the herm of the Spring Equinox marked a moment of transformation? Isn't it the case that this is more the rehearsal of something that is said that he didn't yet understand? So that it is only later, in the arrangement of this last collection that he makes of that earlier moment a transformation in which finally what he *understands* of transformation occurs. That we are both here and not and that in us work the changes that, we might say, angels also perform in their movements towards and away from us. And that this cannot be said except in these consoling transpositions.

* * *

The third section of the book brings us up time and presents some 13 poems from late winter and early spring 1924. These date to the months following the collapse of his health in November 1923 and his first extended stay at the Valmont sanatorium. The tone of these is stark; there is perhaps a new awareness that spring might be numbered that creeps into what is otherwise traditional pastoral praise. And, in keeping with what I've traced above, the time is doubled—the poems collect around the spring equinox and move forward in relation to the "autumn" that begins the collection, and yet we are also back in time (in the spring *before* the poems at the outset), still moving *towards* a present that has already been cited.

In keeping now with the sequence of time proper to this third set, the poems from late winter and spring are followed by six poems from June 1924—the same June already cited by the set piece 'Nine Poems Written in a Churchyard in Ragaz' that studs the first part of the collection. All but the last of the second set of poems from June 1924 continue the pastoral focus of the poems from winter and spring 1924 and differ in this way from the Churchyard poems. So that, if the Churchyard poems signaled something like the persistence of June as a jewel set into in Autumn, these poems simply cite June as what follows spring, and thus the nevertheless forward movement of time and mortality—a movement undispelled by the otherwise persistence we can also say.

And yet, even here, where he seem to again return to a moment, Rilke breaks us off into the open—the penultimate poem of this second set of six from June 1924 is the great "what birds drop through is not / the intimate affordance that intensifies form for you." This poem tears us out of the pastoral perspective—we are suddenly talking of great things again in the most sophisticated of philosophical diction, and this sets the stage for a last set of ten poems, a set that constitutes something like a testament.

The last set of poems is a "selected" that brings together poems from 1922 and 1925 and concludes with three poems from 1914-5. The arrangement is no longer seasonal—the seasonal cannot hold what Rilke has to say. Instead the set begins with a poem written the night before he began to compose the *Sonnets to Orpheus*. That poem is followed by three studies, 'Idol,' 'Image on a Vase,' and 'Gong' that strangely echo Keats' 'Ode on a Grecian Urn.' These are followed by a poem called 'Warrant' (Vollmacht), a word that has the sense of the charge a dying person might issue his heirs, and one titled 'Advent' that reprises the love poetry of Rilke's—yet unpublished and untranslated—"In Celebration of You' written for Lou Andreas Salomé in 1898.

We're in ritual time now and the order of things is dictated by the respects that must be paid. The thrust of that movement persists where Rilke reaches back again in time and offers the poem 'Antistrophe,' from 1914, originally intended as the Fifth Elegy and thus as the middle and hinge of that set. An antistrophe is, of course, the second, counter movement in the dance of the Greek chorus, whose movement gives us one sense of the movement of a lyric. The antistrophe follows and enacts the sway, the movement back, and the placement here marks a loyalty to the lyric that persist in Rilke's aesthetic instincts and informs the structure of the whole. And even here it is out of step—moved from the middle of one sequence to the end of an other—and yet in that being out of joint, something is completed.

The last two poems—'Lament,' and the untitled "Music: perhaps the breath of statues"—are themselves musical in the sense of according with the energies and momentum Rilke has established. Rilke is, of course, the poet of lament, and yet this last poem breaks away from its title into jubilation. Once again the Angel is cited—here among last things, Rilke is careful to speak of how at last his "Jubel Tree" arrives, ever more beautiful, "in my invisible / landscape, which you, Angel made / known to me, invisible." Because even here Rilke finds it necessary to speak of the inner affordance within which the gesture which becomes realized and consoling tree (realized image) occurs. A movement he won't say is his, that he has to say as Angel (he might have said Martian!).

The last poem is an untitled meditation on music from 1915. The ending is a reprise of this exquisite invisible movement:

> You are a stranger, music. You, the heart's affordance that
> springs open in us. Our innermost, that wells up over us
> pressing us out...., holier parting:
> there the inner surrounds us,
> as the most practiced distance, as a different
> side of the air,
> pure,
> grand,
> no longer habitable.

It breaks off terribly, naming a beyond-which towards which Rilke moves. The beyond-which that is, as Dickinson began to know, out of sequence, that cannot be comprised. A beyond-which that is characteristic of our being here and the kind of creature we are, looking out into a open which is both a further and a breaking off into which we literally are lost, dying, persistent perhaps as a June recalled in Autumn, where color does not stop.

* * *

Poets have many readers, and we read according to where we are in the music of things, according to the time of life, the conversations that we have or are immersed in, our ways of seeing and our questions about these. I am a reader immersed in discourse on poetics. It's hard for me not to write about Rilke's approach to lyric without Nathaniel Mackey's notion of splay and stagger in the back of my mind, hard for me not to notice that what Rilke seems to say about time foreshadows Eliot's 'Four Quartets' and echoes the eruption of death in Dickinson's art. Others will find other things, and yet the work of these poems, like the work of Dickinson, Eliot, or Mackey, the work of others like these, is a work by which what I've translated as *room* and *affordance* is proffered. It's true that this word could be translated as space, and yet, in Rilke's hands it is only rarely ever an emptiness or a vacuity, it is almost always something that opens out impossibly, like a lotus or rose, that occurs with the force of filling-up we sense when we look up at the night sky and are amazed to find ourselves amidst what we want to call plenitude. In the depths of night, perhaps in death, not as what we can never see but only know in some Platonic sense, but as a visible force that carries in it an invisible never that nevertheless spans open and sparkles above us.

Notes to the Poems

The following notes are offered as commentary and as a supplement to the poems of *From Notebooks and Personal Papers*. For the purposes of space, the German and French for all poems translated here is given in both reduced font and in prose-block stanza notation. All texts are from the 1955 Insel *Sämtliche Werke*.

1. *Herbst / Autumn* (pp. 12–13)

Many of Rilke's collections begin with poems that reprise 'The Entrance' from *Book of Images* (1902). That poem is a study of the way in which an image gets realized; it sets out the key motif of a tree's rise (impossible, against gravity) and spread, a trope to which Rilke will return repeatedly. At stake here is the thought that the image rises in us impossibly much as a tree somehow is drawn upwards and supports itself. While Rilke's interest is in the realized artistic image, his discussion has significance for the way in which images arise in our thoughts and dreams as well.

The second poem, 'Bygone Apollo,' is the first poem of *New Poems* (1907). The poem that begins the second set of New Poems, 'The Archaic Torso of Apollo' is, alongside 'The Panther' perhaps Rilke's best known poem. Both are usefully read as meditations on the conceit of the image— here the image of poet-god—and on the way realization of an image in art produces transformation. The last poem here is the first of the *Sonnets to Orpheus*.

Entrance

Whoever you might be: in the evening, step out
of your rooms, into all that you know;
as though at last your house was set before the far-off:
whoever you might be.
With your eyes, which, barely tired,
free themselves from the worn-out threshold,
you slowly lift a black tree
and place it against the sky: simple, alone.
And you have made the world. And it is huge
and like a word it ripens in silence.
And as your will grasps its meaning,
your eyes tenderly let it go…

SW I, p. 371: Eingang: Wer du auch seist: am Abend tritt hinaus / aus deiner Stube, drin du alles weißt; / als leztes vor der Ferne liegt dein Haus: / wer du auch seist. // Mit deinen Augen welche müde kaum / von der verbrauchten Schwelle sich befrein, / hebst du ganz langsam einen schwartzen Baum / und stellst ihn vor den Himmel: schlank, allein. / Und hast die Welt gemacht. Und sie ist groß / und wie ein Wort, das noch im Schweigen reift. / Und wie dein Wille ihren Sinn begreift, / lassen sie deine Augen zärtlich los…

Bygone Apollo

Just as so often through still barren
branches a morning shines that is the
whole of spring: so, nothing in his
head was able to keep the radiance

of all poems from striking us senseless;
for there was still no shadow in his gaze,
his temples were still too fresh for laurels
and only later would a long-stemmed

rose garden grow out at his eyebrows,
whose leaves, separately, would stir
and wash against the whispers of his mouth,

which here is quiet, unopened and shining,
drinking everything in with just his lips,
as if to allow his song to flood in.

SW I, p. 481. Früher Apollo: Wie manches Mal durch das noch unbelaubte / Gezweig ein Morgen durchsieht, der schon ganz / im Frühling ist: so ist seinem Haupte / nichts was verhindern könnte, daß der Glanz // aller Gedichte uns fast tödlich träfe; / denn noch kein Schatten ist in seinem Schaun, / zu kühl für Lorbeer sind noch seine Schläfe / und später erst wird aus den Augenbraun // hochstämmig sich der Rosengarten heben, / aus welchem Blätter, einzeln, ausgelöst / hintreiben werden auf des Mundes Beben, // der jetzt noch still ist, niegebraucht und blinkend / und nur mit seinem Lächeln etwas trinkend / als würde ihm sein Singen eingeflößt.

From *Sonnets to Orpheus*

I.1

A tree rose there. Oh pure overflow!
Oh! Orpheus sings! Oh taller tree in the ear!
And everything went still. Yet even in that stillness,
a new beginning appeared, a wink and transformation.

Out of the silence, Beasts came through the clear
empty forest   from their lairs and nests;
and showed themselves, and neither out of stealth
nor fear were they themselves so silent,

but because they'd heard. Bellows, shrieks, roars
seemed of no account to their hearts. And where there had been
no more than a hut, in which to find welcome

shelter from the darkest yearnings,
with a rude entranceway, whose posts shook—
there, in their ears, you built a temple for them.

SW I, p. 732: Da steig ein Baum. O reine Übersteigung! / O
hoher Baum im Ohr! / Und alles schweig. Doch selbst in der Verschweigung
/ ging neuer Anfang, Wink und Wandlung vor. // Tiere aus Stille drangen aus
dem klaren / gelösten Wald von Lager und Genist; / und da ergab sich, daß
sie nicht aus List / und nicht aus Angst in sich so leise waren, // sondern aus
Hören. Brüllen, Schrei, Geröhr schien klein in ihren Herzen. Und wo eben /
kaum eine Hütte war, dies zu empfangen, // ein Unterschlupf aus dunkelstem
Verlangen // mit einem Zugang, dessen Pfosten beben,—/ da schufts du ihnen
Tempel in Gehör.

2.
"…Wenn aus des Kaufmanns Hand" / *"…As if a scale is passed"* pp.14–15

Rilke does not cite the figure of the angel often in *Notebooks and Personal
Papers*. The figure of the angel is central to *Poems on the Night* and to
the first two Elegies. By this date, Rilke had developed a sophisticated
angelology that reflected early 2nd- and 3rd-century theological models

within Jewish-Christian circles that were later made doctrine in Islam. The angel was conceived of as a dynamic figure (image) by and through which it was possible to know an otherwise inconceivable God; in this sense the angel was less a guardian-protector than an agent in the process by which God was revealed/humans came to know God. From this perspective, the angelic order is always moving both toward us and toward God and thus is itself a double movement similar to other notions of double movement discussed above. It is of note that Rilke's interest in the figure of the angel in such terms dates to at least the 1913 *Poems to the Night*. During the war years, Rilke would live in Munich next door to Paul Klee, and they were frequent visitors. Klee's work with the motif of the angel dates to this period, and, as many know, Walter Benjamin's 1940 study of the angel of history takes as its starting point Klee's 1920 painting *Angelus Novus* (The New Angel).

There are too many angel poems to cite. I offer two unpublished poems. The first is from *Poems to the Night*—this poem is one of several addressed to a sister-friend and marks the first citation of the angel in the text; the second was written in the weeks leading up to the late Feb 1922 breakthrough when the Elegies were completed and the Sonnets emerged.

Look, throughout the affordance, angels feel
their unstoppable feelings.
Our incandescence would be cool to them.
Look, angels glow throughout the affordances.

Whereas one of we who know no better
defends herself and the other commits to nothing,
they stride, with rapt purpose,
through their appointed regions.

From *Gedichte an die Nacht*, SW II p. 69-70: Siehe, Engel fühlen durch den Raum / ihre unaufhörlichen Gefühle. / Unsere Weißglut wäre ihre Kühle. / Siehe, Engel glühen durch den Raum. // Während uns, die wirs nicht anders wissen, / eins sich wehrt und ein umsonst geschieht, / schreiten sie, von Zielen hingerissen, / durch ihr ausgebildetes Gebiet.

Love, the angel is affordance.
The world's affordance, as if the land grant
of a loving angel, is full
of starry gifts.

We, on wrought nights,
we fall from intimacy to intimacy,
and where the lover melts,
we are a rolling stone.

But here, where we never
find ourselves, are the Angel's affordances.
Feel: in a holy flurry
they blessedly transform in themselves.

SW II, p. 474: Liebe der Engel ist Raum. / Der Weltraum ist wie Gewahrung /
liebender Engel, erfült / von dem gestirnten Geschenk. // Wir in den ringen-
den Nächten / wir fallen von Nähe zu Nähe, / und wo die Liebende taut, /
sind wir ein stürzender Stein. // Aber auch hier wo wir niemals / uns finden,
sind Räume der Engel. / Fühl: in heiligem Eilschritt / wandeln sie selig sich an.
Muzot: Feb. 9th 1922.

3. *"Ach, nicht getrennt sein" / "Ah, not to be separated"* (pp. 16-17)

The "inner" is a key figure for Rilke, used to assert the existence of depth
against the Modernist attention to surface. The first poem translated
below 'Within a Rose' is an apt example of this focus. While surface was
a critical feature for Rilke—his work on Rodin attends to the ways that
an idea is accomplished at and in the play of surfaces—he nevertheless
resisted the impulse to reduce Being to surface, recognizing the "inner"
as a condition or limit we could not ultimately repudiate or negate. See
my essay in *Roses: The Late French Poetry of Rainer Maria Rilke* for more
about this.

   This poem also is one of two (see also poem # 41) that makes use
of the image of the birds being thrown through or dropping through
the open—an image that Rilke finds in the First Elegy (written in 1912)
where he speaks of the birds that fall through the open. I've included two
other poems in which Rilke develops this motif, one from the spring of
1913 (written in Paris after Rilke's stay in Rondo) and one from a short
suite written for Lulu Albert-Lazard in 1914.

Within a Rose
　　From *New Poems: The Other Part* (1908)

Where is there an outside to
this inside? On which wound
does one put such linen?
Which Sky is reflected inside
in the inland lake
of these open roses,
these carefree ones—look:
how they lie, loose in
idleness, as if a shaking hand
could never spill them.
They can hardly stop themselves;
so much departure
overwhelmed and flowed
out from their inwardness
into the days, which, continually
fuller and fuller, come to an end,
until the whole of summer becomes
a room, a room in a dream.

(SW I, pp. 622-3): Wo ist zu diesem Innen / ein Außen? Auf welches Weh /
legt man solches Linnen? / Welche Himmel spiegeln sich drinnen / in dem
Binnensee / dieser offenen Rosen, / dieser sorglosen, sieh: / wie sie lose im
Losen / liegen, als könnte nie / eine zitternde Hand / sie verschütten. / Sie
können sich selber kaum / halten: viele ließen / sich überfüllen und fließen /
über von Innenraum / in die Tage, die immer / voller und voller sich schließen,
/ bis der ganze / Sommer ein Zimmer / wird, ein Zimmer in einem Traum.

Look! I am amazed how nothing
needs a basis or a dependable grip.

The world throws itself in what's free.

Look, what flashes! Look,
a flock of doves
wheels away from more familiar places.

SW II 394: Staune, siehe, wie keines / Boden verlangt und verläßlichen Haltes. // Ins Freie wirft sich die Welt. /.............................. // Sieh, stahlender, sieh / schwenkt sich ein Wurf / Tauben zurück aus dem erprobteren Raum (Morning Sky, Paris, May 1913).

From 'Poems to Lulu Albert-Lazard'

XII

How birds, which live in a
massive bell, in a bell-cage,
suddenly, with resounding feeling,
plunge in the morning air
and in their flight express
the signature
of their beautiful
terror about the scrawled tower:

By these notes, would we know
we cannot stay in our hearts

SW II 224: Wie die Vögel, welche an den großen / Glocken wohnen in den Glockenstühlen, / plötzlich von erdröhnenden Gefühlen / in die Morgenluft gestoßen / und verdrängt in ihr Flüge / Namenszüge / ihrer schönen / Schrecken um die Türme schreiben: // können wir bei diesem Tönen / nicht in unsern Herzen bleiben / .... / .... / *(Munich, Oct 1st 1914).*

> 4. *"Unaufhaltsam, ich will die Bahn vollenden"* /
> *"Ceaselessly, I want to finish this path"* (pp. 18-19)

Rilke wrote many poems in which he attempted to describe the arc of his development in self-mythologizing or psychological terms that pitted him against transformation. An earlier version of this trope from the first section of *Book of Hours*:

I live my life in widening rings,
that cloud *things* over.
I may not in the end accomplish it,
but I'll make the attempt.

I circle around God, around that age-old tower,
I've circled for thousands of years;
and I still don't know: am I a falcon, a storm
or a great song.

SW I p. 253.: Ich lebe mein Leben in wachsenden Ringen, / die sich über die Dinge ziehn. / Ich werde den letzten vielleicht nicht vollbringen, / aber versuchen will ich ihn. // Ich kreise um Gott, um den uralten Turm, / und ich kreise jahrtausendelang; / und ich weiß noch nicht: bin ich ein Falke, ein Sturm / oder ein großer Gesang.

5. *"Falter"* / *"Butterflies"* (pp. 26–27)

The image of the butterflies at Ragaz in June 1924 returns in the short French suite *Les Roses*, written in late September-Early October 1924 while Rilke stayed briefly at a lakeside spa-hotel in Lausanne. Rilke's treatment of the movement of butterflies here is echoed in a separate trope derived from his practice of laying flower petals across his closed eyelids, a motif that he would use for his epitaph: Rose, oh pure difference, joy, / to be No-one's sleep under so many / lids. (Rose, ô reiner Wiedersprach, Lust / niemandes Schlaf zu sein unter soviel / Lidern.)

From *Les Roses* (1926)

II
I see you, rose, book half-opened,
having so many pages
of detailed happiness
we will never read. Mage-Book,

which is opened by the wind and can be read,
eyes shut…
from which butterflies scatter, confused
to have had the same ideas.

SW II p. 575: Je te vois, rose, livre entrebaîllé, / qui contient tant de pages / de bonheur détaillé / qu'on ne lira jamais. Livre-mage, // qui s'ouvre au vent et qui peut être lu / les yeux fermés…, / dont les papillons sortent confus / d'avoir eu les mêmes idées.

VII

Resting, cool bright
rose, against my closed eyes—
one would say a thousand eyelids
were superimposed

against this hot one of mine.
A thousand slumbers against my feigning lids
beneath which I roam
in a fragrant labyrinth.

SW II p. 577: T'appuyant, fraîche claire / rose, contre mon oeil fermé—, / on dirait mille paupières / superposées // contre la mienne chaude. / Mille sommeils contre ma feinte / sous laquelle je rôde / dans l'odorant labyrinthe.

XVIII

All that we feel, you share,
yet we ignore what happens to you.
There would have to be a hundred butterflies
to read all your pages.

There are ones among you like dictionaries;
those who gather these
are tempted to bind all the pages.
Me? I like the roses which are letters.

SW II p. 581: Tout ce qui nous émeut, tu le partages. / Mais ce qui t'arrive, nous l'ignorons. / Il faudrait être cent papillons / pour lire toutes tes pages. // Il y en d'entre vous qui sont comme des dictionnaires; / ceux qui les cueillent / ont envie de faire relier toutes ces feuilles. / Moi, j'aime les roses épistolaires.

In the *Sonnets to Orpheus*, Rilke develops the image of Orpheus as a hermetic summoner and Master. The 1906 poem Goldsmith (see below, note 18) reflects an early version of the figure. In the Sonnets, Rilke depicts the poet-alchemist-god as a being capable of the kind of double movement celebrated in 'Magic.' (See below, note 8). I have also included a poem from a cycle of poems written by Rilke for Lulu Albert-Lazard, a young married woman whom he met in the first days of his flight to Germany at the start of WWI. They had an affair that lasted several years. The poem here serves as a stage for several of the motifs tracked in these notes including the exchange between faces and the thought of birds being thrown through what is immeasurably open.

From *Sonnets to Orpheus*

I.5

Put up no marker. Let roses
bloom each year for his memory.
Orpheus is there. His metamorphosis
in this and that. We should not trouble

with another name. It's the same for all times—
when he sings, it's Orpheus. He comes and goes.
Isn't it already enough, when he sometimes stays on
for a few days longer than the bowl of roses?

O, that he must vanish so that you understand!
And when I, myself, worried for him, he disappeared.
Even as his word reaches past the here and now,

he is already out there, where you cannot follow.
The lyre's frame does not constrain his hand,
And he listens, even as he steps beyond.

SW I 733: Errichtet keinen Denkstein. Laßt die Rose / nur jedes Jahr zu seinen Gunsten blühn. / Denn Orpheus ists. Seine Metamorphose / in dem und dem. Wir sollen uns nicht mühn // um andre Namen. Ein für alle Male

/ ist Orpheus, wenn es singt. Er kommt und geht. / Ists nicht schon viel, wenn er die Rosenschale / um ein paar Tage manchmal übersteht? // O wie er schwinden muß, daß ihrs begrifft! / Und wenn ihm selbst auch bangte, daß er schwände. / Indem sein Wort das Hiersein übertrifft, // ist er schon dort, wohin ihrs nicht begleitet. / Der Leier Gitter zwängt ihm nicht die Hände. / Und er gehorcht, indem er überschreitet.

I.6

Is he someone from around here? No, his broad
nature awoke from both realms.
The one who bends the willow's branches
has heard of the willow's roots.

When you go to bed, leave no bread on
the table, no milk; the dead rise—.
But he, the summoner, would blend,
under your eyelid's yielding,

his appearance into every thing that's shown;
and may the magic of earth-smoke and rue
be as real to him as the clearest strings.

A valid image is not damaged by him;
Be it from the grave or in this room,
he praises the ring, the bangle and jar.

SW I 734: Ist er ein Hiesiger? Nein, aus beiden / Reichen erwuchs seine weite Natur. / Kundiger böge die Zweige der Weiden, / wer die Wurzeln der Weiden erfuhr. // Geht ihr zu Bette, so laßt auf dem Tische / Brot nicht und Milch nicht; die Toten ziehts—. / Aber er, der Beschwörende, mische / unter der Milde des Augenlids // ihre Erscheinung in alles Geschaute; / und der Zauber von Erdrauch und Raute / sei ihm so wahr wie der klarste Bezug. // Nichts kann das gültige Bild ihm verschlimmern; / sei es aus Gräbern, sei es aus Zimmern, / rühme er Fingerring, Spange und Krug.

I.7

It's to praise! He who orders us to praise
came here like ore from the stones'

silence. His heart, o more transient winepress
of an endless vintage for us.

His voice never falls to dust
if a godlike instance seizes him.
All becomes vineyard, all becomes grape,
ripened in his sensitive south.

The decay in the tombs of kings does not
punish him to put aside praising, nor
that a shadow falls from the gods.

He is the just the herald who always remains,
who holds bowls of praiseworthy fruit
still farther through the doors of the dead.

SW I 735: Rühmen, das ists! Ein zum Rühmen Bestellter, / ging er hervor wie
das Erz aus des Steins / Schweigen. / Sein Herz, o vergängliche Kelter / eines
den Menschen unendlichen Weins. // Nie versagt ihm die Stimme am Staube,
/ wenn ihn das göttliche Beispiel ergreift. / Alles wird Weinberg, alles wird
Traube, / in seinem fühlenden Süden gereift. // Nicht in den Grüften, der
Könige Moder / straft ihm die Rühmung lügen, oder / daß von dem Göttern
ein Schatten fällt. // Er ist einer der bleibenden Boten, / der noch weit in die
Türen der Toten / Schalen mit rühmlichen Früchten halt.

I.9

Only he also who truly lifts the
lyre within shadows
is able to reply to
endless laud with foresight.

Only he who ate poppies
with the dead
will never again drop the
slightest note.

The reflection in a lake may
often begin to swim for us:
Realize the image.

Only in the doubled-field
do the voices become
eternal and mild.

SW I 736: Nur wer die Leier schon hob / auch unter Schatten, / darf das
unendliche Lob / ahnend erstatten. // Nur wer mit Toten vom Mohn / aß, von
dem ihren, / wird nicht den leisesten Ton / wieder verlieren. // Mag auch die
Spielung im Teich / oft uns verschwimmen: / *Wisse das Bild.* // Erst in dem
Doppelbereich / werden die Stimmen / ewig und mild.

From 'Poems for Lulu Albert-Lazard'

IV

Is all this ours, Lulu? Is it ours? Or does all this
meet elusive shapes in us?
we hold open our hearts and through them goes
the God with wings at his ankles,

the one, you know, that seizes the poets:
ah, they still understand, by way of their creaturely nature,
that he recognizes them and enraptures them
and declares them to the Immeasurable.

One God only has the power to
untangle what still lacks purpose.
Like the night between two days
he suddenly stands between our lives
lives that are full of hesitating stars.

He calls to us both now as Poet.
And you glow softly and I glow.
And he throws we, who are the birds of his
joy, through the clearings of our faces.

SW II 219: Sind wirs, Lulu, sind wirs? Oder grüßen / sich in uns entgangene
Gestalten? / Durch die Herzen, die wir offen halten, / geht der Gott mit
Flügeln an den Füßen, // jener, weißt du, die Dichter nimmt; eh sie noch
von ihrem Wesen wissen, / hat er sie erkannt und hingerissen / und zum

Unermessenen bestimmt. // *Einem* Gott nur ist die Macht gegeben, das noch Ungewollte zu entwirrn. / Wie die Nacht mit zweien Tagen neben / steht er plötzlich zwischen unsern Leben / voll von zögerndem Gestirn. // In uns beide ruft er nach dem Dichter. / Und da glühst du leise und ich glühe. / Und er wirft uns durch der Angesichter / Klärungen die Vögel seiner Frühe. *(Irschenhausen, Sept 21ˢᵗ 1914)*

7. *"Das (Nicht Vorhandene) Kindergrab mit dem Ball" /*
"A (Non-Existent) Child's Grave with a Ball" (pp. 32–35)

The motif of the ball should be consider alongside this poem in *Sonnets to Orpheus:*

II.7

A few of them, the first playmates of childhood
in the scattered gardens of the city:
how we found each other and shyly delighted each other
and, like a lamb with a page to recite

spoke as though mute. If we were once glad,
it didn't matter. Whose was it?
And how that dissolved in the midst of all the flourishing people
and in the fears of the long year.

Strange carts undid us as they were pulled by,
houses stood stark about us, but false,—and no one
ever knew us. *What* was useful in any of it?

Nothing. Only the balls. Their magnificent arcs.
Not even the children… but sometimes one stepped out
o a vanishing one, under the falling ball.
                    (In Memory of Egon von Rilke)

SW I 755-6: Wenige ihr, der einstigen Kindheit Gespielen / in den zerstreuten Gärten der Stadt: / wie wir uns fanden und uns zögernd gefielen / und, wie das Lamm mit dem redenden Blatt, // sprachen als Schweigende. Wenn wir uns einmal freuten / keinem gehörte es. Wessen wars? / Und wie zergings unter allen den gehenden Leuten / und im Bangen des langen Jahrs. // Wagen

umrollten uns fremd, vorübergezogen, / Häuser umstanden uns stark, aber
unwahr,—und keines / kannte uns je. *Was* was wirklich im All? // Nichts. Nur
die Bälle. Ihre herrlichen Bogen. / Auch nicht die Kinder... Aber manchmal
trat eines / ach ein vergehendes, unter den fallenden Ball.

8. *Magie / Magic* (pp. 38–39)

In the second stanza of this poem, Rilke makes a point that is difficult
to render in English. He says the ordinary word appears *hinausgestuft*,
which has the sense of "tiered" or "set out in tiers" which I render as
layered. In the last two lines of the poem he presents a figure based on
"*Tauber*" (m) and "*Taube*" (f). *Taube* can mean either dove/pigeon, or the
deaf/a deaf person. These two meanings are "layered" in the figure—the
context does not clarify which sense is called for, and both might register
for a reader. Rilke shows something poets discover which is that one can
imbed several images in a single set of words—that a simple word brings
at least two worlds into being as if by magic and at the same time is "real,"
or "workable" in the sense of having a referent/doing what a word does.

The effect Rilke produces here is similar to a kind of poetic language
used in Tantric and Erotic poetry in India called "Twilight Language"
(*sandhyabhasa*) where words are used in ways that create double or coded
referents. This suggests the extent to which Rilke has moved toward the
"both-and" of a non-dual sense of the way language works.

9. *"Welt was in dem Antlitz der Geliebten" /*
"World was in the face of the beloved" (pp. 44–45)

The notion of the lover's face and, more generally, the idea of "face" is
one Rilke returned to repeatedly from the 1902 *Book of Images* through
Poems to the Night. A face was, frequently, the device by which a radical
difference was introduced, a difference that was not reducible and that
was, in some way, self-defining. In, for instance, 'People in the Night,'
Rilke uses candlelit faces to establish a difference between the lonely night
streets (and the space there) and a sudden intimate and claustrophobic when
confrontation with the other that occurs when when goes indoors and
sits with strangers by candlelight. In *Malte Laurids Brigge,* Rilke considers when?
the facelessness of the urban dweller when he describes a woman who,
when she lifts her face from her hands is faceless, having left "the last

of her faces" in her hands. In the material from the 1906 Capri Journal we see that Rilke also used the notion of face (and of our having several faces) with respect to himself and in speaking to a young correspondent about self-knowledge and the work of becoming someone.

People at Night

The nights are not made for the crowd.
The night separates you from your neighbor,
and you should not search for him in any case.
At night, you light your room
to look at the faces of the people there,
and you think: whose are these?

The people are terribly distorted by the light that
dribbles off their faces—
at night they merge together,
so you see a single, wavering world,
heaped up in confusion.
A yellow glow on their brow
has driven away all thoughts,
wine flickers in their eyes,
heavy gestures weigh
their hands, they use these to make
themselves understood as they speak;
and by doing this they say: *I* and *I*
and *mine*: Whoever they are.

SW I 392 Menschen bei Nacht: Die Nächte sind nicht für die Menge gemacht. / Von deinem Nachbar trennt dich die Nacht, / und du sollst ihn nicht suchen trotzdem. / Und machst du nachts deine Stube licht, um Menschen zu schauen ins Angesicht, / so mußt du bedenken: wem. // Die Menschen sind fruchtbar vom Licht entstellt, / das von ihren Gesichtern träuft, / und haben sie nachts sich zusammengestellt, / so schaust du eine wankende Welt / durcheinandergehäuft. / Auf ihren Stirnen hat gelber Schein / alle Gedanken verdrängt, / in ihren Blicken flackert der Wein, / an ihren Händen hängt / die schwere Gebärde, mit der sie sich / bei ihren Gesprächen verstehn; / und dabei sagen sie: *Ich* und *Ich* / und meinen: Irgendwen.

From *Poems to the Night*

Were I to feed on your face
as tears do when crying,
my brow, my face would breed
around the breaths that I meet in you,
....

SW II 73: Wenn ich so an deinem Antlitz zehre / wie die Träne an dem
Weinenden, / meine Stirne, meinen Mund vermehre / um die Züge, die ich an
dir kenn, ...

Once, I took your face in both
my hands. The moon fell across it.
Even more inconceivable than moonlight, *a separate
face that looks back* under overflowing weeping.

As if something willing, that becomes still,
it was almost like a *thing* you'd hold.
And yet, in this cold night, no
creaturely form more endlessly eludes me.

O, we stream toward this Place,
press into it's smallest folds,
all the waves of out hearts, the
desire and weakness—
and, in the end, who is it that we hold off?

Alas, it's the foreign, misunderstood by us,
alas, the other, which we never found,
the servants, that are bound for our sake,
the spring winds that vanished around us,
and the quiet, the losers.

SW II 72: Einmal nahm ich zwischen meine Hände / dein Gesicht. Der Mond
fiel darauf ein. / Unbegreiflichster der Gegenstände / unter überfließendem
Gewein. // Wie ein williges, das still besteht, / beinah war es wie ein Ding zu
halten. / Und doch war kein Wesen in der kalten / Nacht, das mir unendlicher
entgeht. // O da strömen wir zu diesen Stellen, / drängen in die kleine

Oberfläche / alle Wellen unsres Herzens, / Lust und Schwäche, / und wenn halten wir sie schließlich hin? // Ach dem Fremden, der uns mißverstanden, / ach dem andern, den wir niemals fanden, / denen Knechten, die uns banden, / Frühlingswinden, die damit entschwanden, / und der Stille, der Verliererin.

From the Second Elegy:

Lovers, you who are enough for each other, I ask
you about us. You clasp yourselves. Do you have proof?
Look, it seems to me that my hands become
aware of each other, or that my worn
face protects itself within them. That gives me a slight
sensation. But who would dare to *be* because of that?
But you, you who wax in the delight of the
other, until he, overwhelmed,
begs you, "no more"—, you who become
more generous yourself under his hands, like a year of grapes;
you who sometimes disappears, just because the other
has taken you over completely; I ask you about us. I know,
you touch each other so blissfully because a caress preserves,
since the stars do not fade, what you tender ones
pull the covers over; because under there, you feel pure
duration. So you almost promise each other eternity
in the embrace. And yet, when the first
second of terror passes and the longing at the window,
and the first outing together, *a single* pass through the Garden:
Lovers, *are* you still what you were? When one of you lifts the
other to his mouth and fixes you with a kiss—: drink on drink:
o, how the action of drinking strangely slips away.

SW I 691: Liebende, euch, ihr in einander Genügten, / frag ich nach uns.
Ihr greift euch. Habt ihr Beweise? / Seht, mir geschiehts, daß meine Hände
einander / inne werden oder daß mein gebrauchtes / Gesicht in ihnen sich
schont. Das giebt mir ein wenig / Empfindung. Doch wer wagte darum schon
zu *sein*? / Ihr aber, die ihr im Entzücken des anderen / zunehmt, bis er euch
überwältigt / anfleht: nicht *mehr*—; die ihr unter den Händen / euch reichlicher
werdet wie Traubenjahre; die ihr manchmal vergeht, nur weil der andre / ganz
überhand nimmt: euch frag ich nach uns. / Ich weiß, / ihr berührt euch so
selig, weil die Liebkosung verhält, / weil die Stelle nicht schwindet, die ihr,
Zärtliche, / zudeckt; weil ihr darunter das reine / Dauern verspürt. So versprecht
ihr euch Ewigkeit fast / von der Umarmung. Und doch, wenn ihr der ersten

/ Blicke Schrecken besteht und die Sehnsucht am Fenster, / und den ersten gemeinsamen Gang, *ein* Mal durch den Gärten: Liebende, *seid* ihrs dann noch? Wenn ihr einer dem andern / euch an den Mund hebt und ansetzt—: Getränk an Getränk: / o wie entgeht dann der Trinkende seltsam der Handlung.

10. *"Gestirne der Nachte, die ich erwachter gewahre"/*
"Stars of the night that, waking, I begin to see" (pp. 48–49)

Rilke's work on the night sky and, in particular, his awareness that the night sky was never an absolute dark but always studded by the stars made him sensitive to the notion of form as constellation—a thought that dates at least to Mallarmé's notion of constellated form in 'Un coup de dés.' For a discussion of the latter see Dee Reynolds (Dee Reynolds. *Symbolist Aesthetics and Early Abstract Art*. Cambridge Studies in French 51. Cambridge University Press, 1995). The idea that a new art would somehow involve the realization of new constellations is developed in the Sonnets. It is of note that the German custom of capitalizing nouns produces the surface effect of producing a text that is "constellated"— organized around the slightly brighter (stresses) stars that establish the terms of the semantic relations of the poem.

From *Sonnets to Orpheus*

I.11

Look at the sky. Is there no constellation called "Rider?"
For, it is printed strangely on us:
this proud heraldic badge of the earth. And a second,
that rushes at him and holds him, that he carries.

Isn't it so? That the sinewy nature of being
is to be chased and subdued?
Path and Change. And yet a mark makes this intelligible.
A new expanse. And the two are one.

But *are* they there? Or, for me are both
the path, which they are on together?
Indeed, the nameless distinguish them as table and meadow.

But the starry connection is deceptive.
And yet for now, this moment frees us
to think of the figure. That's enough.

SW I 737-8: Sieh den Himmel. Heißt kein Sternbild "Reiter"? / Denn dies
ist uns seltsam eingeprägt: / dieser Stolz aus Erde. Und ein Zweiter, / der ihn
treibt und halt und den er trägt. // Ist nicht so, gejagt und dann gebändigt,
/ diese sehnige Natur des Seins? / Weg und Wendung. Doch ein Druck
verständigt. / Neue Weite. Und die zwei sind eins. // Aber *sind* sie's? Oder
meinen beide / nicht den Weg, den sie zusammen tun? / Namenlos schon
trennt sie Tisch und Weide. // Auch die sternische Verbindung trügt. / Doch
uns freue eine Weile nun / der Figur zu glauben. Das genügt.

I.20

But for you, Lord, o what can I devote to you or say,
who taught all creation how to listen.?—
I remember, on the first day of spring,
in the evening, in Russia—, a horse…

Here from the village came a white horse, all alone,
a stake tied around his front fetlock,
to be free out in the fields for the night;
how the curls of his mane beat

against his neck with the pulse of his spirits,
in spite of that uneven, hampered gallop.
How the springs of horse-blood leapt!

Who felt the open, and it's question!
Who sang and heard—your cycle of myths
was closed in him.
     His image: my offering.

SW I 743-4: Dir aber, Herr, o was weih ich dir, sag, / der das Ohr den
Geschöpfen gelehrt?—/ Mein Erinnern an einen Frühlingstag, / seinen
Abend, in Rußland—, ein Pferd… // Herüber vom Dorf kam der Schimmel
allein, / an der vorderen Fessel den Pflock, / um die Nacht auf den Wiesen
allein zu sein; / wie schlug seiner Mähne Gelock // an den Hals im Takte des
Übermuts, / bei dem grob gehemmten Galopp. / Wie sprangen die Quellen
des Rossebluts! // Der fühlte die Weiten, und ob! / Der sang und der hörte—,
dein Sagenkreis / war *in* ihm geschlossen. / Sein Bild: ich weih's.

11. *"Nacht. Oh du in Tiefe gelöstes"* / *"Night. O you, unfolded in the deep"* (pp. 52–53)

From Poems to the Night see also:

The squandered stars in the flooded sky
splendor over these troubles. Laid back on my pillows,
I cry upwards. Here, on the always weeping,
at the face's limits,
so as to take this in, the ec-
static felt-affordance of the world begins. If you are
drawn out there, what could interrupt
the current? Nothing at all. It's then that
you would suddenly struggle in the enormous pull
of the planets about you. Breathe.
Breathe in the darkness of the earth and again
look up! Again. From the depths above, humbly,
with no heaviness it leans down towards you. The unfolded
night-containing face has room for you.

SW II 54: Überfliessende Himmel verschwendeter Sterne / prachten über
der Kümmernis. Statt in die Kissen, / weine hinauf. Hier, an dem weinenden
schon, / an dem endenden Antlitz, / um sich greifend, beginnt der hin- /
reißende Weltraum. Wer unterbricht, / wenn du dort hin drängst, die
Strömung? Keiner. Es sei den, / daß du plötzlich ringst mit der gewaltigen
Richtung / jener Gestirne nach dir. Atme. / Atme das Dunkel der Erde und
wieder / aufschau! Wieder. Leicht und gesichtlos / lehnt sich von oben Tiefe dir
an. Das gelöste / nachtenthaltne Gesicht giebt dem deinigen Raum.

Whether I once was or am, you stalk
past me, you endless darkness of the light.
And I take the sublime, that Concealer that
you give to the affordances, into my fugitive face.

Night, o would you respond, as I look at you,
as my creaturely being retreats at your approach,
so that it was strengthened and I might dare to throw myself at you?
Would I trust it then, so that the doubly withdrawn brow
would rise above the rivers of these upward glances?

May it be Nature. May it be only *one*
boldly united Nature: this life and over there,
each of the planets that shape us, to whom I ignorantly cry:
o, so will I practice, calmly like a stone,
to be in your pure figure.

SW II 66: Ob ich damals war oder bin: du schreitest / über mich hin, du
unendliches Dunkel aus Licht. / Und das Erhabene, das du im Raume
bereitest, / nehm ich, Unkenntlicher, an mein flüchtig Gesicht. // Nacht, o
erführest du, wie ich dich schaue, / wie mein Wesen zurück im Anlauf weicht,
/ daß es sich dicht bis zu dir zu werfen getraue; / faß ich es denn, daß die
zweimal genommene Braue / über solche Ströme von Aufblick reicht? // Sei
es Natur. Sie es nur *eine* / einige kühne Natur: dieses Leben und drüben jenes
gestalte Gestirn, das ich unwissend anweine: / o so will ich mich üben, gefaßt
wie die Steine / zu sein in der reinen Figur.

12. *"Täglich stehst du mir steil vor dem Herzen"*/ *"Each day you stand above me, steep before the heart"* (pp. 56–61)

The motif of wandering, abandoned in the mountain wilds recurs in
Rilke's work, most notably in a poem written in Sept. 1914 after he'd
been forced to leave Paris and, for several weeks, stayed at a hotel in
Irchenhausen. A slightly different version using the first image as title is
numbered among the suite of poems written in Irschenhausen for Lulu
Albert-Lazard.

Abandoned in the mountains of the heart. See, how nothing is there,
see: the last village of words, and higher,
where there is nothing but the last
farmstead of a feeling. Do you know it?
Abandoned on the mountains of the heart. Stoney ground
under the hands. Surely, something could
bloom here; in the silent ruins
an unknown herb blooms, singing out.
But the one that found it? Alas, he began to know of it
and now stops, abandoned on the mountains of the heart.
Surely he goes, to cure his self-awareness,
somewhere around here, some kind of refuge-seeking mountain
animal, changes and stays. And the huge, hidden bird

circles the peak of pure refusal.—Though
exposed, here in the mountains of the heart.

SW II 94: Ausgesetzt auf den Bergen des Herzen. Siehe, wie klein dort, / siehe:
die letzte Ortschaft der Worte, und höher, / aber wie klein auch, noch ein
letztes / Gehöft von Gefühl. Erkennst du's? / Ausgesetzt auf den Bergen des
Herzens. Steingrund / unter den Händen. Hier blüht wohl / einiges auf; aus
stummen Absturz / blüht ein unwissendes Kraut singend hervor. / Aber der
Wissende? Ach, der zu wissen begann / und schweigt nun, ausgesetzt auf den
Bergen des Herzens. / Da geht wohl, heilen Bewußtseins, / manches umher,
manches gesicherte Bergtier, / wechselt und weilt. Und der große geborgene
Vogel / kreist um der Gipfel reine Verweigerung.—Aber / ungeborgen, hier auf
den Bergen des Herzen…

From 'Poems to Lulu Albert-Lazard'

Exposed on the Heart's Mountains…

Once again the scents of the valleys came to
the one who waited, who struggled in the mountains
of his heart. And he drank the last
breaths, the way the night drinks in the winds.
Stood and drank the scents, drank and knelt
for a while.
Over his stony fields
stood the valley of the breathless
sky. The stars did not pick out
an abundance that anyone's hands could carry,
they processed in silence, like something one had
only heard of, across this weeping face.

SW II 220: Einmal noch kam zu dem Ausgesetzten, / der auf seines Herzens
Bergen ringt, / Duft der Täler. Und er trank den letzten / Atem wie die Nacht
die Winde trinkt. / Stand und trank den Duft, und trank und kniete / noch
ein Mal. / Über seinem steinigen Gebiete / war des Himmels atemloses Tal /
ausgestürzt. Die Sterne pflücken nicht / Fülle, die die Menschenhände tragen,
/ schreiten schweigend, wie durch Hörensagen / durch ein weinendes Gesicht.
(Irschenhausen, Sept 22nd, 1914)

13. *"so viele Dinge liegen aufgerissen"* / *"so many things lie torn open"* (pp. 66–67)

Throughout the work on *New Poems*, Rilke mediated his inquiry into the relationship between image and sensed object through a consideration of what we might call "the-thing-as-such." I italicize *thing* in translation to stress that when Rilke uses this term he is making an argument and/or considering the nature of the sense world and its claims on us. Rilke came to critique any objectivist program as both actually impossible (because of our creatureliness) and as ethically questionable (because we refuse our entanglement in being by imagining/enacting an objective self-position). This is a particularly significant note for readers whose poetics is rooted in the American objectivist impulse, as Rilke's critique, however due, is rarely considered.

14. *Gong* / *Gong* (132–133)

In Rilke's *Complete Works*, there is a French poem 'Gong' written in Paris in 1925 for Suzanne Bertillon, as well as an additional fragment dated to Oct 1925.

Gong
        (for Suzanne B…)
1.

A faint resonance, corrupted silence,
everything that was here, changes into a thousand sounds,
leaves us and returns: strange reconciliation
of the tides of infinity.

One has to close one's eyes and give up speech,
stay mute, blind, dazzled:
the place is utterly shook, what touches us
only wants to listen to our being.

Who is it that suffers? The ear's slight depth
is quickly overwhelmed—, and doesn't one lean
himself against it, completely full of all the sounds,
the vast conch that is the world's ear?

2.

Its as if one were in the midst
of melting bronze gods
in order to again supplement
the massive gods, all gold,
that were undone by the resonance.
And all the Gods that would give themselves
to the flaming metals
would raise the final, royal
sounds.

3.

(…trees of bronze that, in the ear,
  would ripen the round fruit
of their sonorous season…)

SW II 617-8: 1) Bourdonnement épars, silence perverti, / tous ce qui fut
autour, en mille bruits se change, / nous quitte et revient: rapprochement
étrange / de la marée de l'infini. // Il faut fermer les yeux et renoncer (à) la
bouche, / rester muet, aveugle, ébloui: / l'espace tout ébranlé, qui nous touche
/ ne veut de notre être que l'ouïe. // Qui suffirait? L'oreille peu profonde /
déborde vit—, et ne penche-t-on / contre la sienne, pleine de tous les sons /
la vaste conque de l'oreille du monde? // 2) Comme si l'on était en train /
de fondre des Dieux d'airain, / pour y ajouter encor / des Dieux massifs, tout
en or, / qui en bourdonnant se défont. / Et de flambants métaux, / s'élèvent
d'ultimes sons / royaux! // 3) (… Arbres d'airain, qui dans l'ouïe font / mûrir
les fruits ronds / de leur sonore saison…)

Gong

Klang—no longer fathomed by
the ear. As though to be the note
that rings out beyond us,
a ripeness in the affordance.

SW II 506: Klang, nichtmehr mit Gehör / meßbar. Als wäre der Ton, / der uns
rings übertrifft, / eine Reife des Raumes.

15. *Ankunft / Advent* (136–137)

For the repeated motifs of Rilke's love poetry, see:

from 'In Celebration of You' (dedicated to Lou Andreas Salomé)

Even though the hours separate us again :
we are always together in dream
as if under a flowering tree.
We will forget the words said out loud
and will talk about ourselves like a star about a star,—
all the words we said forgotten :
as if under a flowering tree.

SW III 174: Ob auch die Stunden uns wieder entfernen: / wir sind immer
beisammen in Traum / wie unter einem aufblühenden Baum. / Wir werden die
Worte, die laut sind, verlernen / und von uns reden wie Sterne von Sternen,—/
alle lauten Worte verlernen: / wie unter einem aufblühenden Baum.

My life is like a quiet sea:
grief lives in houses on the shore,
it doesn't dare to leave its bounds.
It just sometimes shakes a bit between approach and flight :
disturbed wishes pull it about
around like silver seagulls.

And then all is again silent…
And do you know what my life wants,
have you understood it well?
Like a wave in morning's sea
it wants, resounding and thick-muscled,
to break upon your soul.

SW III 174-5: Mein Leben ist wie leise See: / Wohnt in den Uferhäusern das
Weh,/ wagt sich nicht aus den Höfen. / Nur manchmal zittert ein Nahn
und Fliehn: / aufgestörte Wünsche ziehn / darüber wie silberne Möven. //
Und dann ist alles wieder still… / Und weißt du was mein Leben will, / hast
du, es schon verstanden? / Wie eine Welle im Morgenmeer / rauschend und
muschelschwer, / an deiner Seele landen.

* * *

The beech wood calls quietly.
Waves with its tender branches
far out into the meadows silence.

Will my blonder darling come soon
to show me the deep paths
where the lights are like circling elves?

Will my blonder darling come soon?

A greeting will make my soul bend.
My soul is a solitary bunch of wildflowers
as if in the calling beech wood.

SW III 175: Leise ruft der Buchenwald. / Winkt mit seinen jungen Zweigen
/ weit hinaus ins Wiesenschweigen. // Kommt mein blonder Liebling bald /
mir die tiefen Wege zeigen, / wo die Lichter wie Elfen reigen? // Kommt mein
blonder Liebling bald? // Grüßend wird meine Seele sich neigen. / Meine Seele
ist maieneigen / wie der rufende Buchenwald.

From *Poems to the Night*:

When you came here at midnight,
didn't I breathe in such tidal currents
out of desire for you?
Even as I hoped to still your face in
its almost unslaked splendor
as it rested against mine for a bit
and was filled with endless questions.
to be big enough for your great eyes, the space
about us became silent with my breaths;
I became a mirror, I was drawn down into my blood.

When, through a pale screen of olive trees,
night swayed over me with its stronger stars,
I stood up, stood and bent
backwards and came to recognize
what I could never later recollect for you.

Oh, so much expression was sown into me
that when each of your smiles lifts up I
see out across a whole world-space towards you.
But then you don't come, or you come later.

Throw yourselves, Angels, over these blue
flax fields.   Angels, Angels, reap what's there.

SW II 70: Atmete ich nicht aus Mitternächten, / daß du kämest einst, um
deinetwillen, / solche Flutung? / Weil ist hoffte, mit fast ungeschwächten /
Herrlichkeiten dein Gesicht zu stillen, / wenn es in unendlicher Vermutung /
einmal gegen meinem über ruht. / Lautlos wurde Raum in meinem Zügen; /
deinem großen Aufschaun zu genügen, / spiegelte, vertiefte sich mein Blut. //
Wenn mich durch des Ölbaums blasse Trennung / Nacht mit Sternen starker
überwog, / stand ich aufwärts, stand und bog / mich zurück und lernte die
Erkennung, / die ich später nie auf dich bezog. // O was ward mir Ausdruck
eingesät, daß ich, wenn dein Lächeln je gerät, / Weltraum auf dich überschaue.
/ Doch du kommst nicht, oder kommst zu spät. // Stürzt euch, Engel, über
dieses blaue / Leinfeld. Engel, Engel mäht.

16. *Antistrophes / Antistrophes* (pp. 138–141)

Rilke's use of the image of a young female playmate and, more generally,
his praise of the wise sister-friend takes many forms including the figure
of the young lament in the 10th Elegy and in the Sonnets. This figure
appears to function both in relation to intimate feminine friendships
(with Lou Andreas-Salomé and the Princess Maria) but also in relation
to some notion of an "inner woman" Rilke admitted himself to imagine.
It is well-known that both the final version of the Elegies and Sonnets to
Orpheus were composed under the impact of having heard of a young
woman's death, and the Sonnets, more generally, admit the conceit that
links that young woman and Eurydice. Psychologically inclined readers
have noted that Rilke was born just after his mother had lost a daughter,
and Rilke himself writes about how his mother and he played a game
where she called him by his dead sister's name.

From *Sonnets to Orpheus*

I.2

And it was almost a girl and came forth
out of that lucky break of song and lyre
and shone clear through her spring-time veils
and made herself a bed in my ear.

And slept within me. And her sleep was everything.
The trees that constantly astonished me, the
marked distances, the meadows I longed for,
every wonder that touched my heart.

She slept the world. Singing God, how did you
perfect her so that she wants nothing
but to be awake? Look, she arose and slept.

Where is her death? O will you devise
this motive only when your song is spent?—Where does
she go, as she sinks away from me? ...almost a girl...

SW I 731-2: Und fast ein Mädchen wars und ging hervor / aus diesem einigen
Glück von Sang und Leier / und glänzte klar durch ihre Frühlingsschleier / und
machte sich ein Bett in meinem Ohr. // Und schlief in mir. Und alles war ihr
Schlaf. / Die Bäume, die ich je bewundert, diese / fühlbare Ferne, de gefühlte
Wiese / und jedes Staunen, das mich selbst betraf. // Sie schlief die Welt.
Singender Gott, wie hast / du sie vollendet, daß sie nicht begehrte, / erst wach
zu sein? Sieh, sie erstand und schlief. // Wo ist ihr Tod? O, wirst du dies Motiv
/ erfinden noch, eh sich dein Lied verzehrte?—// Wo sinkt sie hin aus mir? ...
Ein Mädchen fast ...

I.25

But I want *you* now, you whom I knew
like a flower whose name I didn't have,
to remember one more time and to show them, stolen one,
the beautiful playmate of these insurmountable cries.

Just a dancer, who suddenly stopped your so hesitant
body, as though someone had cast your youth in bronze;

grieving and listening—. There, from powers on high,
music fell into your transposed heart.

The illness was near. Already taken over by shadows,
your blood rose, darkening, though, as if just a bit suspicious,
it pulsed with your nature's Springtime.

Again and again, broken by darkness and collapse,
it gleamed, earthly. Until after an awful throbbing,
it stepped through the hopelessly open door.

SW I 747: *Dich* aber will ich nun, *Dich*, die ich kannte / wie eine Blume, von
der ich den Namen nicht weiß, / noch *ein* Mal erinnern und ihnen zeigen,
Entwandte, / schöne Gespielin des unüberwindlichen Schrei's. // Tänzerin erst,
die plötzlich, den Körper voll Zögern, / anhielt, als göß man ihr Jungsein in Erz;
/ trauernd und lauschend—. Da, von den hohen Vermögern / fiel ihr Musik
in das veränderte Herz. // Nah war die Krankheit. Schon von den Schatten
bemächtigt, / drängte verdunkelt das Blut, doch, wie flüchtig verdächtigt, / trieb
es in seinen natürlichen Frühling hervor. // Wieder und wieder, von Dunkel
und Sturz unterbrochen, / glänzte es irdisch. Bis es nach schrecklichem Pochen /
trat in das trostlos offene Tor.

II.12

Desire transformation. O, hunger for the flame
in which a thing withdrawn into you shines in its changes;
what had been sketched as spirit, that now masters the earthly
loves nothing in the figure's flourish more than the turning point.

He who is trapped in staying surely *is* paralyzed;
does he think himself safe in the cover of obtrusive grays?
Standpoint—a hard thing warns of the greatest hardships in the distance
You regret it—: the far-off hammer is lifted!

He who pours himself out from his source gets recognized by Wisdom;
and she takes him, delighted, through the cheerful work
that so often concludes with creation and begins with ending.

Every lucky bit of room is a child or grandchild of parting, where
those two passed, amazed. And Daphne, in the midst of shifting shape,

feels herself become laurel and wants you to change yourself into wind.

SW I, 758-9: Wolle die Wandlung. O sei für die Flamme begeistert / drin
sich ein Ding dir entzieht, das Verwandlungen prunkt; / jener entwerfende
Geist, welcher das Irdische meistert, / liebt in dem Schwung der Figur nichts
wie den wendenden Punkt. // Was sich ins Bleiben verschließt, schon ists das
Erstarrte; / wähnt es sich sicher im Schutz des unscheinbaren Grau's? / Warte,
ein Härtestes warnt aus der Ferne das Harte. Wehe—: abwesender Hammer
holt aus! // Wer sich als Quelle ergießt durch das heiter Geschaffne, das mit
Anfang oft schließt und mit Ende beginnt. // Jeder glückliche Raum ist Kind
oder Enkel von Trennung, / den sie staunend durchgehn. Und die verwandelte
Daphne / will, seit sie lorbeern fühlt, daß du dich wandelst in Wind.

II.18

Dancer: oh you who transpose
all departure with a step: how you brought it here.
And the pirouette at the end, that tree in motion,
didn't it take the circle of the year, utterly, as its own?

Didn't the tree's crown suddenly bloom with stillness, as your
whirling just now crowded in on it? And above it,
wasn't there sunlight, wasn't there summer, warmth,
this endless warmth that poured out from you?

But it also was laden, it was laden, your tree of ecstasy.
Aren't they its peaceful fruits: a pitcher, the potter's
ripening strokes, and an even more ripened vase?

And in the pictures: don't the gestures remain,
the darker stroke of your brow
rapidly sketched on the screen of each turn?

SW I 763: Tänzerin: o du Verlegung / alles Vergehens in Gang: wie brachtest
du's dar. / Und der Wirbel am Schluß, dieser Baum aus Bewegung, / nahm
er nicht ganz in Besitz das erschwungene Jahr? // Blühte nicht, daß ihn dein
Schwingen von vorhin umschwärme, / plötzlich sein Wipfel von Stille? Und
über ihr, / war sie nicht Sonne, war sie nicht Sommer, die Wärme, / diese
unzählige Wärme aus dir? // Aber er trug auch, er trug, dein Baum der Ekstase.
/ Sind sie nicht seine ruhigen Früchte: der Krug, / reifend gestreift, und die

gereiftere Vase? // Und in den Bildern: ist nicht die Zeichnung geblieben, / die deiner Braue dunkler Zug / rasch an die Wandung der eigenen Wendung geschrieben?

II.28

Oh, come and go. Though still almost a child, may you
for a moment complete the figures
in the clear constellation of each dance
by which we briefly surpass dumb, ordinary,

Nature. Because she stirred and
just listened so intently when Orpheus sang.
From then until now you have been troubled
and slightly bothered when a tree pondered

too long about going with you into listening.
You still knew the place where the song
lifted its notes—; the unyielded center.

For you tried the most beautiful steps
and hoped to one day turn towards the unbroken
festival of your friends' gait and countenance.

SW I, pp. 769-70: O komm und geh. Du, fast noch Kind, ergänze / für einen Augenblick die Tanzfigur / zum reinen Sternbild einer jener Tänze, / darin wir die dumpf ordnende Natur // vergänglich übertreffen. Denn sie regte / sich völlig hörend nur, da Orpheus sang. / Du warst noch die von damals her Bewegte / und leicht befremdet, wenn ein Baum sich lang // besann, mit dir nach dem Gehör zu gehn. / Du wußtest noch die Stelle, wo die Leier / sich tönend hob—; die unerhörte Mitte. // Für sie versuchtest du die schönen Schritte / und hofftest, einmal zu der heilen Feier / des Freundes Gang und Antlitz hinzudrehn.

17. *Klage / Lament* (pp. 142–143)

Contrast the sense of resolution in the late poem, 'Lament,' with the following draft for the 10th Elegy, portions of which date to the Duino breakthrough (and retain it's lack of closure) and then revised after Rilke's sojourn in Spain in the winter of 1912-13.

Fragment of the 10ᵗʰ Elegy

That, one day at the gate of grim insight, I might
sing out jubilation and praise to the approving angel.
That none of the clearly striking hammers of the heart
might fail where it glances off or doubts or because of
the furious strings. That my streaming face might make me
more dazzling; that these shy tears might
blossom. O, how dear to me then you would be, you grief-
wracked nights. But I didn't kneel longer with you, heartbroken sisters,
I gave up, I didn't let myself become even further lost
in your loosened hair. We are wastrels of pains.
How we see them ahead as a sad duration.
as if perhaps they won't end, But they are really
our moments, our winter-
long foliage, the meadows, ponds, our innate landscape,
with animals in the reeds and nesting birds.

Up above, on high, doesn't half the sky stand
over the melancholy by which we troubled Nature?
Think! wouldn't you no longer get into your overgrown self-pity,
no longer see the stars through the dry leaves of
pain's blackish foliage, and wouldn't the debris of fate
no longer proffer the spreading moonlight on high,
so that you would sense yourself within, as a people did in the past?
There'd be more smiles too, the consuming ones of those
you forsook at this time or that—, with so little trouble,
the pure ones stepped into your pain even as they simply passed.
(Almost a girl, that justly receives her suitor,
because he has pressured her for weeks, and, frightened, she leads him
to the garden trellis, this man, who rejoices and reluctantly
departs: then she spoils this step towards a fresher farewell,
and she waits and stands and there transposes her fully-present mien
into the look of a stranger, the look of a young lady
who appreciates him endlessly, who is set apart from he who had
                                                    determined her,
apart from this wandering Other, who defines her forever.
He passes by, reverberating.) So you were always lost;
as if you owned nothing: like someone dying,

bent over in the dank, wind-tossed, March night,
alas, spring fades away in the throats of birds.

Often you listened too far into your suffering. You would forget
the slightest of the boundlessly distressing shapes,
would call, cry out, hoping with fresh curiosity,
to come together here with an Angel, whose arduous, darkening expressions
pain-undoing, ever willing,
once described your sobs to you.
Angel, what was that like? And he would imitate you and would not
understand that it was pain, the way someone who takes the
shape of a calling bird fills himself with its innocent voice.

SW II 64: Daß ich dereinst, an dem Ausgang der grimmigen Einsicht / Jubel
und Ruhm aufsinge zustimmenden Engeln. / Daß von den klar geschlagenen
Hämmern des Herzens / keiner versage an weichen, zweifelnden oder /
jähzornigen Saiten. / Daß mich mein strömendes Antlitz / glänzender mache;
daß das unscheinbare Weinen / blühe. O wie werdet ihr dann, Nächte, mir
lieb sein, / gehärmte. Daß ich euch knieender nicht, untröstliche Schwestern,
/ hinnahm, nicht in euer gelöstes / Haar mich gelöster ergab. Wir Vergeuder
der Schmerzen. / Wie wir sie absehn voraus in die traurige Dauer, / ob sie nicht
enden vielleicht. Sie aber sind ja / Zeiten von uns, unser winter- / währiges
Laubwerk, Wiesen, Teiche, angeborne Landschaft, / von Geschöpfen im Schlif
und von Vögeln bewohnt. // Oben, der hohen, steht nicht die Hälfte der
Himmel / über der Wehmut in uns, der bemühten Natur? / Denk, du beträtest
nicht mehr dein verwildertes Leidtum, / sähest die Sterne nicht mehr durch das
herbere Blättern / schwärzlichen Schmerzlaubs, und die Trümmer von Schicksal
/ böte dir höher nicht mehr der vergrößernde Mondschien, / daß du an ihnen
dich fühlst wie ein einstiges Volk? / Lächeln auch wäre nicht mehr, das zehrende
derer, die du hinüberverlost —, so wenig gewaltsam, / eben an dir nur vorbei,
traten sie rein in dein Leid. / (Fast wie das Mädchen, das grade dem Freier sich
zusprach, / der sie seit Wochen bedrängt, und sie bringt ihn erschrocken / an
das Gitter des Gartens, den Mann, der frohlockt und ungern / fortgeht: da stört
sie ein Schritt in dem neueren Abschied, und sie wartet und steht und da trifft
ihr vollzähliges Aufschaun / ganz in das Aufschaun des Fremden, das Auschaun
der Jungfrau, / die ihn unendlich begreift, den draußen, der ihr bestimmt war, /
draußen den wandernden Andern, der ihr ewig bestimmt war. / Hallend geht er
vorebei.) So immer verlorst du; / als ein Besitzender nicht: wie sterbend einer, /
vorgebeugt in die feucht herwehende Märznacht, / ach den Frühling verliert in
die Kehlen der Vögel. // Viel zu weit gehörst du in's Leiden. Vergäßest /
du die geringste der maßlos erschmerzten Gestalten, / riefs du, schrieest, hoffend auf
frühere Neugier, / einen der Engel herbei, der mühsam verdunkelten Ausdrucks

/ leidunmächtig, immer wieder versuchend, / dir dein Schluchzen damals, um jene, beschriebe. / Engel wie wars? Und er ahmte dir nach und verstünde / nicht daß es Schmerz sei, wie man dem rufenden Vogel / nachformt, die ihn erfüllt, die schuldlose Stimme. *Duino 1912 & Paris end of 1913*

18. *"Musik" / "Music"* (pp. 144–145)

The following is the last entry in Rilke's *Notebook*, and dates toward the middle of December 1926.

You come, you at last, whom I acknowledge—
more hopeless pain in this bodily web:
as if I burned in spirit, see, I burn
in you; the wood has long resisted,
the flame that you would light in response
but now I feed you and in you I burn.
In your grip, my familiar mildness becomes
an alien hellish fury.
Utterly pure, utterly without purpose and free of any future, I
climb onto the jumbled pyre of suffering,
so certain that this heart whose last reserves burn
has nothing with which to bargain for any future anywhere.
Am I now that unrecognizable thing that burns there?
I can snatch no memories from it.
O life, life: exposed being.
And I in conflagration. No one knows this about me.

To be abandoned. It is not like being sick once
was in childhood. Then it was deferment. An excuse
to grow even greater. Everyone murmured and cheered.
Don't confuse this with what first astonished you.

SW II 511: Komm du, du letzter, den ich anerkenne, / heilloser Schmerz im leiblichen Geweb: / wie ich im Geiste brannte, sieh, ich brenne / in dir; das Holz hat lange widerstrebt, / der Flamme, die du loderst, zuzustimmen, / nun aber nähr' ich dich und brenn in dir. / Mein hiesig Mildsein wird in deinem Grimmen / ein Grimm der Hölle nicht von hier. / Ganz rein, ganz planlos frei von Zukunft stieg / ich auf des Leidens wirren Scheiterhaufen, / so sicher nirgend Künftiges zu kaufen / um dieses Herz, darin der Vorrat schwieg. / Bin ich es noch, der da unkenntlich brennt? / Erinnerungen reiß ich nicht herein. / O Leben, Leben: Draußensein. / Und ich in Lohe. Niemand der mich kennt. // [Verzicht. Das ist nicht so wie Krankheit was / einst in der Kindheit. Aufschub. Vorwand um / größer zu werden. Alles rief und raunte. / Misch nicht in dieses was dich früh erstaunte.

On "Raum":
Non-dual Experience, Translation and Affordance

Raum (space, perhaps room in the sense of the space for or around something) is a key word in Rilke's lexicon, often used in compounds such as *Weltraum* (world-space) or *Zwischenraum* (between-space) to anchor relations or dynamics that otherwise appear to lack a ground or field. A good deal of Rilke scholarship treats Rilke's use of *raum* as a reflection of either a late-Romantic or early Modernist concern with negation as an ultimate or critical ground, thus arguing for the persistence of a dialectical movement in Rilke's lyric. That is, they read Rilke to be concerned with the problem of radical negation as a movement in dialectical process and believe his pathos to be a pathos of alienation and/or a celebration of what negation affords.

My approach to Rilke's use of the term differs. While I agree that Rilke places considerable force on the term—a force comparable perhaps only to the stress he places on "thing"—by 1912 Rilke had begun to revise his understanding of self and world in light of both the lessons of his work on *New Poems* and on the emergence of a non-dual perspective that would become central to his poetics. Hence, from this time, Rilke increasingly uses the term not to celebrate negation but to turn *our* reading of negation in light of or toward a non-dual understanding of self and world.

One of the problems occasionally faced by translators is that in any language there are a range of dictions and technical argot so that a word like "space" or "ground" belongs to and can be read as referring to several discursive *topoi*. For instance, "ground" can be used in unreflective reference as a reference to dirt or soil, or the ground floor, but the same term is used in philosophical or logic to refer to a thing's basis, what establishes it and so on. While the relationship between these uses may (as Lakoff and Johnson say) be metaphorical, the analogy on which the usage is based is arbitrary and conventional. In the example, the coherence of the usage in logic is based on having selected *one* feature of ground—its being under us—to the exclusion of others—its constant erosion, its being subject to weather, its flint or clay paucity and need for nutrients to be arable, and so on.

The translator working on poetry and mystical literature has an additional problem in that poetic and mystical language often works with *and* against the grain of cultural logic and/or makes use of the overlap between two discursive *topoi* to reopen the question of how the worlds of the imagination and of sense might be related. Whether the reader makes the leap or not, a poet who writes "ground is not ground" may be saying several things at once, and close reading is required to trace these out. In such cases, the translator has to be careful to decide whether the effect is best reproduced by staying true to ordinary language equivalents or whether something more must be done.

The challenge is even sharper in the context of writing that may be influenced by the emergence of a non-dual perspective, as for instance, in the context of Buddhist Perfection of Wisdom literature and tantric poetry. That said, in these two cases, the term non-dual is one of several used to characterize an institutionalized view or method of reading by which a non-ordinary mode of reading is proposed, one that somehow gets at the way things are without an appeal to metaphysical categories. But non-dual thought is by no means the *property* of these traditions, and the term is currently used more widely where a critic hopes to suggest a poet's language works beyond what a simple dialectic would allow, whether the poet is influenced by a particular cultural iteration of this or not.

It is relation to this last that some familiarity with the history of Buddhist discourse on the non-dual interpretation of world is nevertheless relevant as it is one of the few places where we have a sustained critical discourse about non-dual language. What that discourse suggests—in its varied iterations in India, Tibet and East Asia—is both the persistence of a tendency to think non-dual in monist terms as if non-dual referred to an experience in which everything appears as one, and the recurrence of a critique of this. For instance, in Buddhist descriptions of insight into the fact that self and other lack (are empty of) ultimate ground, this experience is described as being as if self and object are "poured into each other"—as if one had poured water into water, as if to say in the end that there was *no difference* to be discerned. Some Buddhist thinkers appear to take this quite strongly as suggesting that a single undifferentiated field of being/awareness is opened out (in which self and object do not appear); others properly point out that to think such a field as any apparitional lack of differentiation is to think in binary terms of presence and absence. The issue is particularly pertinent because Buddhist discourse uses the language of emptiness with respect to ultimate truth, *and this is often read as if asserting some real emptiness, like the emptiness inside a pot, some "not being there" that exists as the ground of and in relation to illusory appearance.*

In Buddhist discourse, the problem with this is that to think this way is to still think in dualist, binary terms of presence and absence. Hence, alongside the persistence of assertions that appear to suggest an actual emptiness or oneness, one finds key Buddhist thinkers consistently critiquing this as inapt, and insisting that a non-dual perspective refutes nothing that exists. What this means in terms of presence and absence is that the relationship between appearance and emptiness—between the appearance of a difference between myself and world and the absence of such a difference—*cannot be that of a dialectic in which emptiness is the negation of appearance.* That is, non-dual is *not* strictly speaking "the assertion of one instead of two," but rather the decision to think appearance by a different means than the *binary* logic of presence and absence, i.e, non-dual because not thought according to a binary.

While it is not possible to say that Rilke had the kind of insight characterized in Buddhist texts as non-dual, it is possible to trace a movement in his thoughts towards a view that is consistent with a critique of identity and language in non-dual terms. This movement begins in the midst of his efforts to overcome subjective distance in the *New Poems* and ends in the *Sonnets to Orpheus* with the assertion that the living and dead exist in different but not bifurcated realms. While the *Duino* breakthrough of 1912 was a critical turning point, the evidence that Rilke's critique of the *New Poems* project was leading him toward a non-dual perspective lies elsewhere—specifically in the unpublished collection *Poems to the Night* and in the prose essay 'Experience,' written in 1912, but published in two parts in 1912. Only Part I was published during Rilke's lifetime (in 1919); they were first published together in 1938.

The received biography of Rilke's life and the development of his poetics treats the years following the publication of *New Poems II* in 1908 through the beginning of WWI as a period of crisis marked by the Duino breakthrough but also by reflection on the costs and conceits of his approach to art and life. The *New Poems* project had depended on a hope that it would be possible for an artist to so empty self as to become such a transparent instrument that one could then render a thing directly without the distortions of subjective distance. As an aesthetic discipline, the hope to so mute self that some Other could be present in its own terms might have benefits; as a method for getting at the way things are however, it would only be reliable if, in fact, it were possible or consistent with the way things are to mute the self in this way—that is, if self were an actual absence that could be filled and then emptied. Otherwise, to think this way would represent an idealized notion—a position extent only in the imagination.

In the poem 'Turning,' written in the summer of 1914, Rilke offers a critique of this approach. There he judges himself in the third person as one who had looked intently at things but had lacked love. The "turn" of the poem involves the charge to henceforth look at things with love, an approach that can only be accomplished if one befriend his "inner woman." The suggestion here is that the discipline assumed for the *New Poems* places the artist in a relation to things that is not unlike that of the objective observer who looks on but is not at stake. Whether possible or not—the suggestion is that its at least possible to act *as if* such a relation was possible—Rilke rejects the discipline on ethical terms as both hyper-masculine and as a position lacking love. What led him to this?

For Rilke, the effort to self-empty had taken many forms including a traditional renunciate fear of romantic entanglement. Though he had married in 1901 and had a child, he claimed the right to live apart and made much of an artist's right to solitude. In the months leading up to the Duino breakthrough, Rilke had at last settled the terms of his divorce from Clara Westhoff (the divorce wouldn't be finalized until 1919, but the terms were set in 1911). The divorce was happening, however, at a time when Rilke had begun to question whether his posture of self-abjection was livable. While it is true that Rilke never wholly resolved his fears of romantic entanglement, by 1914 he would again attempt to "be in love," and there is a new frank acceptance of his sexual nature signaled both in the Third Elegy (completed in late autumn 1913) and the erotic suite 'Seven Poems' written for Lulu Albert-Lazard in late autumn 1915. In the context of Rilke's varied self-conceits and the relationship of these to his creative work, the perhaps forced self-critique of his conduct in his marriage and the recognition of the *limits* of the conceit of selflessness that informed the *New Poems* appear to occur coincidentally and might well have been isomorphic. A key to both would be a reevaluation of the extent of any possible renunciation and, in formal terms, a reevaluation of negation.

During the winter of 1913, Rilke worked on and finalized a manuscript, *Poems to the Night,* in which he explicitly took up the great Romantic trope for a field of radical foundational and consoling negation. Novalis' *Hymns to the Night* was written shortly after the death of the poet's beloved and attempts to counter death by a redemptive celebration of the night (as a field of radical negation) as an ultimate ground of being.

While Novalis' approach is consistent with some negative theology that stresses the radical difference of what saves, its conclusions depend on a binary of light and dark, presence and absence and, significantly, depend on an idealist delineation of night rather than one based on the way night gives itself to sense. In *Poems to the Night*, Rilke takes up night as trope, but he takes it up in what we might call realist terms—night is not delineated according to a logic that finds it to be the opposite of day, but rather in accordance with the ongoing life of the senses which find the night to be full of breezes and shadows and stars, streetlamps and houses, a lover's face on a pillow, a sister in the dark—full that is of appearance, hardly without light, different and magical but not this way according to a logical binary of presence and absence, but in the same way as any of life—day or night—is different and magical.

If we read night here as a trope for negation, then the collection finds a negation that is not categorical—the not-day is not categorically "not-day" but simply a time of reduced light, paired with and equal to the day, but not its other—a time of strangeness perhaps, but not a time that is categorically other. And, the relationship Rilke finds he has with world is not changed by the transition from night to day, so night is not a different ground of being counterposed to day. It will take Rilke another nine years, but in 1922, he will phrase the difference between life and death in the same way, hoping like Novalis to counter the fear and loss we face in death, but doing this in non-dual rather than idealist, categorical terms.

The work of 1912-1914 thus points to a shift in Rilke's ethics that hinged on a critique of the idea that he could somehow exist apart from or free of his embodiment, both because there was no ground of pure absence (pure non-appearance) and because of the claims sexuality made on him and the ethical costs of this. In terms of what has been said here about a non-dual perspective, to think self absent as Rilke had tried to do for *New Poems* would be to still think self and other in binary terms, and the work of this period suggests he had begun to realize a different view was necessary. We don't know if a thorough shift to think in non-dual terms had occurred, but we know he'd at least recognized that Novalis' effort to think the night as a radical absence was not apt.

How then is all this reflected in my translation of *raum*? While in general, I prefer to use ordinary language equivalents in translation, I do translate *raum* variously, and I do so in relation to the shifts I outline above. In writing that dates prior to 1911 and especially where the reference seems ordinary, I render *raum* as "space. In subsequent writing I use "room" and "affordance" as these are closer to his critique of negation and the conceit of self-emptying, and closer to the fact that in later work, *raum* is not an emptiness but something that makes room *for*.

In *Roses: The Late French Poetry of Rainer Maria Rilke*, I delineated the ways in which Rilke uses *raum* to refer to something like "room for or of," so that *Weltraum* is less "the space around a world" and thus "Outer Space" (as it is nowadays colloquially) than that field which is a world's appearance, that external field of appearances which we construe as world, and so on—a space or room or emptiness that is also the appearance which occurs in and in terms of its scope. While as an equivalent, "room" has the virtue of its rhyme, it's not possible to use rhyme as the basis for transposing the music of one language to another—for the most part I aim at reproducing cadence and strive to distribute something like the weight of the syllable from one language to the next—in this volume I've used "affordance" as a way to get at the way Rilke turns "*raum*" in his later poetry. It is a strong choice, but so many readers and critics think "space" refers to an actual emptiness or void, and so the choice seems warranted.

* * *

While we don't know whether Rilke had an experience that formed the basis of his shift to thinking in non-dual terms, and while we can trace a movement toward a non-dual perspective in the logic of self-critique limned above, the short prose piece 'Experience,' written in late winter 1912 (after the Duino breakthrough) does offer Rilke's descriptions of a kind of experience that may have functioned as a warrant for his thought. In the first part of the piece, Rilke relates an experience he'd had while wandering the grounds about Duino. Leaning against a tree, he found himself plunged into a subtle mode of altered awareness that he then describes. As he does so, he struggles to find ways of describing the degree to which everything in his surroundings appeared richly present to him even as he became sensitive to infinitely subtle vibrations of these that were "erupting in him." He wondered if he had gotten fully out into that Other we speak of as Nature, into what he would later call "the Open." But, if this is the open, if it is a mode of awareness in which the difference between self and other has collapsed, it is not a mode of awareness for which the *conventions* of differentiating between interior and exterior *topoi* are inapt. Far from losing any sense of difference, he feels difference more keenly and as a mode of reciprocity, and he says this.

In the second part of the piece, Rilke links the Duino experience to other similar moments, including one that had occurred in Capri in 1906 where a bird-call had plunged him into a reverie in which his intense inwardness was for once not felt as separation from what he sensed. He goes on to say that these experiences set him apart from others, placing him in relation to "a capaciousness so little proper to the human that they would not call it anything other than 'the void' (*Leere*)." Rilke does not use the word *leere* (empty) frequently—he uses it far less often than *raum,* and nowhere else does he come close to glossing *raum* as *leere.* Where *leere* is used it marks a poverty, something unwanted, and actual abandonment. In this passage, he contrasts the insight he has to the ways ordinary people see things. Hence, when he says others would call what he sees "the void," he doesn't mean it *is* a void; he means that this is what they would call it.

Why would others call this "the void?" In the context again of Buddhism, it is well known that a critique of identity often leads to the conclusion—still mediated by binary thought—that if there is no self, then according to a logic of presence and absence this must mean that what exists is an absence that is empty of self. I once sat through an instruction of no self that demonstrated that no intrinsically extant hand existed anywhere. The teacher laughed a bit and asked, "where then is the hand?" I and others were thinking "well, there is no hand anywhere" at which point he slapped himself on the head with his hand! No hand doesn't mean no hand! It means that there is no hand that exists in binary terms. Hence, we speak of no self as "the void" or as an emptiness only because we cannot think yet in terms other than binary, and the binary terms of Being allow us to think only of presence and absence.

Whether Rilke understood this thoroughly or not, what he says in this essay is a close parallel. Folks who don't yet see would call what he sees "the void;" they would try to think negation as he had, in logical terms, and they wouldn't yet see what he had, by virtue of an experience that was not of "nothing" or even indescribable, but rather involved an intensification of his sense of being at stake in Being.

Experience

[I]

It must be a little more than a year ago since something uncanny befell him in the gardens of a castle that rather steeply sloped down to the sea. Having gone out with a book open as was his habit, he had gone there to lean against the roughly shoulder-high fork of a shrubby tree, and right away he felt so pleasantly supported and so amply withdrawn, that he, not reading, completely set into the countryside, lingered in this way in an almost unconscious reverie. Little by little, his attentiveness was roused by a feeling he'd never known: it was as if suddenly imperceptible vibrations had been transmitted to him from within the tree; he was set against it without a care, so that nothing else was visible—perhaps a gentle sweeping wind came to the slope from the woods to show it off, as though it needed an encore, so that the trunk seemed to be strong, appearing so firm despite so little labor. What was powerfully at work in him was not, however, a consideration of this or something of a similar sort; rather, he was more and more astonished, yes, moved by the effects, the indistinct penetrating-from-without that erupted in him: he never thought he'd be fulfilled by quieter movements, it was like his body had become a cared-for soul and, set in that stance, had achieved such a degree of influx that further clarity of more truly physical proportions could not have been found. It happened that he could not, with his first look, properly ascertain the sensation, because of which, he received a communion that seemed fine and extended; there was also a state that this communion gave form to in him; it was so perfect and incessant, different from all others, but hard to believe in because the intensity went beyond anything experienced before, that he could not compare it with any other delicacy so as to say it was pleasing to him. Nevertheless, making an effort, so as to at least give an account, he strenuously wondered what had happened to him, he asked himself: had he gotten to the other side of Nature? As in a dream sometimes, so this phrase brought joy to him now, and he held it to be almost completely applicable. Everywhere and always more symmetrically, he felt repeated pulsing throngs with this, in strange internal intervals; his body became indescribably sensitive but still capable despite that, clear and carefully poised, precise as a revenant, that, dwelling elsewhere, comes in melancholy to what it had previously put aside, there once again, although dispersed, to listen to the once so truly indispensable world. Looking slowly around himself, so as not to disturb himself from his stance, he discerned everything, remembered it, as if he'd smiled at it with a more remote affection, gently afforded it attention, as if in a time just a bit earlier, in circumstances now past, it had been of interest to him. He looked closely at a bird, a shadow caught his attention, even the bare path, as if he was walking along it and was lost, filled him with pensive attention that seemed so much purer than he'd otherwise known. He had not been able think of any such repose, so that he *returned* to all this that was just here, to this body, looking out, as if into the depths of a forgotten window: he took a few seconds longer to satisfy himself thus, so that the sudden appearance of companion would have had the most painful effect on him, though he truly, in his Nature, was prepared for that, to see Polyxène or Raimondine or some other now deceased member of the house step out from the winding of the paths. He grasped the superfluity of his form, it gave him confidence to see what that what the earthly educated thought so absolutely fugitive was useful, the coherence of its usefulness drove everything else he'd been taught from him; he was certain, under its movements, that nothing would befall him. A periwinkle stood near him and every now and then confronted him with its blue glance, coming up to touch him across his spiritual remove, but with such inexhaustible significance that it could no longer hide. Altogether he was able to perceive things as if everything that stood before him was more remote and somehow gave itself more truly, that it might lay in his glance, that was no longer directed onwards and was rarified there, in the open: he looked, as if over his shoulder, back at *things*, and from them arose, what for his isolated spirit, was a bolder sweeter aftertaste than had ever come, full-bodied, from the scent of the blossoms of parting.—Telling himself from this moment to the next, that this could not last, he nevertheless was not afraid of the cessation of this extraordinary state, as if for him, much as with music, just a ceaselessly more patterned, rhythmic opening out was to be expected.

Suddenly his position began to bother him, he felt the trunk, the weariness of the book in his hand, and came to. A stronger breeze rustled now in the tree, it came up from the sea, the bushes rooted into the slope and tangled amongst each other.

Later he intended to remember certain moments in which the power of this one was really condensed, as in a seed. He thought about a time in that other southerly garden (in Capri); there'd been a bird-call far off, and in his inwardness there was an answering, in which, so to speak, he did not burst the bounds of his body; there both call and his inwardness were gathered into a single uninterrupted room, in which, mysteriously protected, there remained just a solitary place of purest, deepest awareness. At that time, he closed his eyes so as not to be disturbed in the generous experience by the contours of his life-body, and it happened that the endlessness of every direction companionably passed into him, so that he was could think to feel the light pressure of the erstwhile appearing stars in his breast.

Another time, how much he'd felt flow out of him, when he'd leaned in a quite similar reverie against a fence to see the star-studded sky through the gentle branches of an olive tree, how face-like the world's affordance facing him was in this this mask, or how, when he'd endured this long enough, everything opened out in welcome in the clear resolution of his heart, so that the scent of creation was in his creaturely being. He'd held it to be possible that he could reflect on such devotions as far back as in his stifling childhood; he just had to recall the passion, that had continually gripped him, when he was permitted to face a storm, how he, striding across a vast plain and aroused in his innermost places, broke through the perpetually re-arising wall of wind that faced him, or how, standing on a ship facing out, he was carried blindly through the dense far-off that closed fast behind him. But if, from the beginning to now, the elemental down-rush of the wind, the pure and varied behaviors of the water, and the heroic progress of the clouds seized him up out of the crowd, yes him, who never was able to grasp in human terms what had stepped into his soul as if it were, in reality, fate, so it couldn't escape him, that he was then, after that last influx, to be surrendered to such, let's call them, relationships. Some kind of gentle tenancy was sustained between him and people, a pure, almost actualized in-between-space, through which perhaps a few individuals were allowed to reach, which just absorbed each circumstance in itself and, brimmed with that, the way a duller smoke makes it hard to tell shape from shape. He still didn't know how his isolation seemed to others. As far as he could tell, at first it gave him a certain freedom to move among people—the hesitant forays of poverty, for which he was more relaxed, gave him a certain agility in relation to they whose hopes and anxieties involved each other, in relation to this knot of death and life. The temptation was still within him, to counter there complaints with his leisure, even though he recognized well, how he deceived them by this, since they could not really understand that he had not (unlike the hero) reached the kind of bridge he had come to in relation to entanglements with them, nor in relation to the dark stirrings of their hearts, but to something beyond, to a capaciousness so little proper to the human that they would not call it anything other than "the void." All that he could make of this for them was likely that he was simple; to speak to them of joy remained stored-up in him, as he found them quite partial in regards to the opposite of happiness, and similarly he had not yet told them something about his acquaintance with nature, about *things*, which they had neglected or had just considered incidental.

German Text of 'Experience'

Erlebnis

I

Es mochte wenig mehr als ein Jahr her sein, als ihm im Garten des Schlosses, der sich den Hang ziemlich steil zum Meer hinunterzog, etwas Wunderliches widerfuhr. Seiner Gewohnheit nach mit einem Buch auf und abgehend, war er darauf gekommen, sich in die etwa schulterhohe Gabelung eines strauchartigen Baumes zu lehnen, und sofort fühlte er sich in dieser Haltung so angenehm unterstützt und so reichlich eingeruht, daß er so, ohne zu lesen, völlig eingelassen in die Natur, in einem beinah unbewußten Anschaun verweilte. Nach und nach erwachte seine Aufmerksamkeit über einem niegekannten Gefühl: es war, als ob aus dem Innern des Baumes fast unmerkliche Schwingungen in ihn übergingen; er legte sich das ohne Mühe dahin aus, daß ein weiter nicht sichtlicher, vielleicht den Hang flach herabstreichender Wind im Holz zur Geltung kam, obwohl er zugeben mußte, daß der Stamm zu stark schien, um von einem so geringen Wehen so nachdrücklich erregt zu sein. Was ihn überaus beschäftigte, war indessen nicht diese Erwägung oder eine ähnliche dieser Art, sondern mehr und mehr war er überrascht, ja ergriffen von der Wirkung, die jenes in hin unaufhörlich Herüberdringende in ihm hervorbrachte: er meinte nie von leiseren Bewegungen erfüllt worden zu sein, sein Körper wurde gewissermaßen wie eine Seele behandelt und in den Stand gesetzt, einen Grad von Einfluß aufzunehmen, der bei der sonstigen Deutlichkeit leiblicher Verhältnisse eigentlich gar nicht hätte empfunden werden können. Dazu kam, daß er in den ersten Augenblicken den Sinn nicht recht feststellen konnte, durch den er eine derartig feine und ausgebreitete Mitteilung empfing; auch war der Zustand, den sie in ihm herausbildete, so vollkommen und anhaltend, anders als alles andere, aber so wenig durch Steigerung über bisher Erfahrenes hinaus vorstellbar, daß er bei aller Köstlichkeit nicht daran denken konnte, ihn einen Genuß zu nennen. Gleichwohl bestrebt, sich gerade im Leisesten immer Rechenschaft zu geben, fragte er sich dringend, was ihm da geschehe, und fand fast gleich einen Ausdruck, der ihn befriedigte, vor sich hinsagend: er sei auf die andere Seite der Natur geraten. Wie im Traume manchmal, so machte ihm jetzt dieses Wort Freude und er hielt es für beinah restlos zutreffend. Überall und immer gleichmäßiger erfüllt mit dem in seltsam innigen Abständen wiederkehrenden Andrang, wurde ihm sein Körper unbeschreiblich rühend und nur noch dazu brauchbar, rein und vorsichtig in ihm dazustehen, genau wie ein Revenant, der schon anderswo wohnend, in dieses zärtlich Fortgelegtgewesene wehmütig eintrat, um noch einmal, wenn auch zerstreut, zu der einst so unentbehrlich genommenen Welt zu gehören. Langsam um sich sehend, ohne sich sonst in der Haltung zu verschieben, erkannte er alles, erinnerte es, lächelte es gleichsam mit entfernter Zuneigung an, ließ es gewähren, wie ein viel Früheres, das einmal, in abgetanen Umständen, an ihm beteiligt war. Einem Vogel schaute er nach, ein Schatten beschäftigte ihn, ja der bloße Weg, wie er da so hinging und sich verlor, erfüllte ihn mit einem nachdenklichen Einsehn, das ihm umso reiner vorkam, als er sich davon unabhängig wußte. Wo sonst sein Aufenthalt war, hätte er nicht zu denken vermocht, aber daß er zu diesem allen hier nur *zurückkehrte*, in diesem Körper stand, wie in der Tiefe eines verlassenen Fensters, hinübersehend:—davon war er ein paar Sekunden lang so überzeugt, daß die plötzliche Erscheinung eines Hausgenossen ihn auf das qualvollste erschüttert hätte, während er wirklich, in seiner Natur, darauf vorbereitet war, Polyxène oder Raimondine oder sonst einen Verstorbenen des Hauses aus der Wendung des Weges heraustreten zu sehn. Er begriff die stille Überzähligkeit ihrer Gestaltung, es war ihm vertraut, irdisch Gebildetes so flüchtig unbedingt verwendet zu sehn, der Zusammenhang ihrer Gebräuche verdrängte aus ihm jede andere Erziehung; er war sicher, unter sie bewegt, ihnen nicht aufzufallen. Eine Vinca, die in seiner Nähe stand, und deren blauem Blick er wohl auch sonst zuweilen begegnet war, berührte ihm jetzt aus geistigerem Abstand, aber mit so unerschöpflicher Bedeutung, als ob nun nichts mehr zu verbergen sie. Überhaupt konnte er merken, wie sich alle Gegenstände ihm entfernter und zugleich irgendwie wahrer gaben, es mochte dies an seinem Blick liegen, der nicht mehr vorwärts gerichtet war und sich dort, in Offenen, verdünnte; er sah, wie über die Schulter, zu den Dingen zurück und ihrem, für ihn abgeschlossen Dasein kam ein kühner süßer Beigeschmack hinzu, als wäre alles mit einer Spur von der Blüte des Abschieds würzig gemacht.—Sich sagend von Zeit zu Zeit, daß dies nicht bleiben könne, fürchtete er gleichwohl nicht das Aufhören des außerordentlichen Zustands, als ob von ihm, ähnlich wie von Musik, nur ein unendlich gesetzmäßiger Ausgang zu erwarten sie.

Auf einmal find seine Stellung an, ihm beschwerlich zu sein, er fühlte den Stamm, die Müdigkeit des Buches in seiner Hand, und trat heraus. Ain deutlicher Wind blätterte jetzt in dem Baum, er kam vom Meer, die Büsche den Hang herauf wühlten in einander.

II

Späterhin meinte er, sich gewisser Momente zu erinnern, in denen die Kraft dieses einen schon, wie im Samen, enthalten war. Er gedachte der Stunde in jenem anderen südlichen Garten (Capri), da ein Vogelruf draußen und in seinem Innern übereinstimmend da war, indem er sich gewissermaßen an der Grenze der Körpers nicht brach, beides zu einem ununterbrochenen Raum zusammennahm, in welchem, geheimnisvoll geschützt, nur eine einzige Stelle reinsten, tiefsten Bewußtseins blieb. Damals schloß er die Augen, um in einer so großmütigen Erfahrung durch den Kontur seines Leibes nicht beirrt zu sein, und es ging das Unendliche von allen Seiten so vertraulich in ihn über, daß er glauben durfte, das leichte Aufruhn der inzwischen eingetretenen Sterne in seiner Brust zu fühlen.

Auch fiel ihm wieder ein, wie viel er darauf gab, in ähnlicher Himmels durch das milde Gezweig eines Ölbaums hindurch gewahr zu werden, wie gesichthaft in dieser Maske der Weltraum ihm gegenüber war, oder wie, wenn er Solches lange genug ertrug, Alles in der klaren Lösung seines Herzens so vollkommen aufging, daß der Geschmack der Schöpfung in seinem Wesen war. Er hielt es für möglich, daß, bis ins eine dumpfe Kindheit zurück, solche Hingegebenheiten sich würden bedenken lassen; mußte er doch nur an die Leidenschaft erinnert werden, die ihn immer schon ergriff, wo es galt, sich dem Sturm auszusetzen, wie er auf großen Ebenen schreitend, im Innersten erregt, die fortwährend vor ihm erneute Windwand durchbrach, oder vorn auf einem Schiffe stehend, blindlings, sich durch dichte Fernen hinreißen ließ, die sich fester hinter ihm schlossen. Aber wenn, von Anfang an, das elementarische Hinstürzen der Luft, des Wassers reines und vielfältiges Benehmen und was Heroisches im Vorgang der Wolken war, ihn über die Maßen ergriff, ja ihm, der es im Menschlichen nie zu fassen vermochte, recht eigentlich als Schicksal an die Seele trat, so konnte ihm nicht entgehen, daß er nun, seit den letzten Einflüssen, solchen Beziehungen gleichsam endgültig übergeben sei. Etwas sanft Trennendes unterhielt zwischen ihm und den Menschen einen reinen, fast scheinenden Zwischenraum, durch den sich wohl Einzelnes hinüberreichen ließ, der aber jedes Verhältnis in sich aufsaugte und, überfüllt davon, wie ein trüber Rauch Gestalt von Gestalt betrog. Noch wußte er nicht, wie weit den Anderen seine Abgeschiedenheit zum Eindruck kam. Was ihn selbst anging, so verlieh erst sie ihm eine gewisse Freiheit gegen die Menschen,—der kleine Anfang von Armut, um den leichter war, gab ihm unter diesen aneinander Hoffenden und Besorgten, in Tod und Leben Gebundenen, eine eigene Beweglichkeit. Noch war die Versuchung in ihm, ihrem Beschwerten sein Leichtes entgegenzuhalten, obwohl er schon einsah, wie er sie darin täuschte, da sie ja nicht wissen konnten, daß er nicht (wie der Held) in allen ihren Bindungen, nicht in der schweren Luft ihren Herzen, zu seiner Art Überwindung gekommen war, sondern draußen, in einer menschlich so wenig eingerichteten Geräumigkeit, daß sie sie nicht anders als "das Leere" nennen würden. Alles, womit er sich an sie wenden durfte, war vielleicht seine Einfalt; es bleib ihm aufbewahrt, ihnen von der Freude zu reden, wo er sie zu sehr in den Gegenteilen des Glücks befangen fand, auch wohl ihnen einzelnes aus seinem Umgang mit der Natur mitzuteilen, Dinge, die sie versäumten oder nur nebenbei in Betracht nahmen. (SW VI 1036-1042).

CPSIA information can be obtained
at www.ICGtesting.com
Printed in the USA
BVHW030220071118
532413BV00001B/74/P

9 781848 616028